Flower Mandalas Workbook
(Mandala Coloring Books For Adults)

Grown-Ups Color Therapy Book
For Meditation & Relaxation

Zen Journal Team

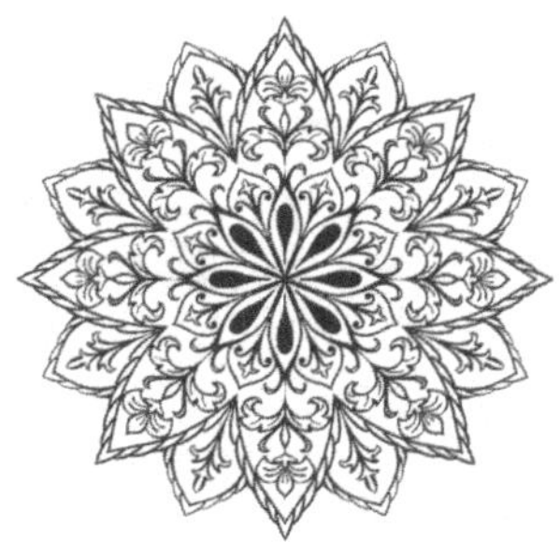

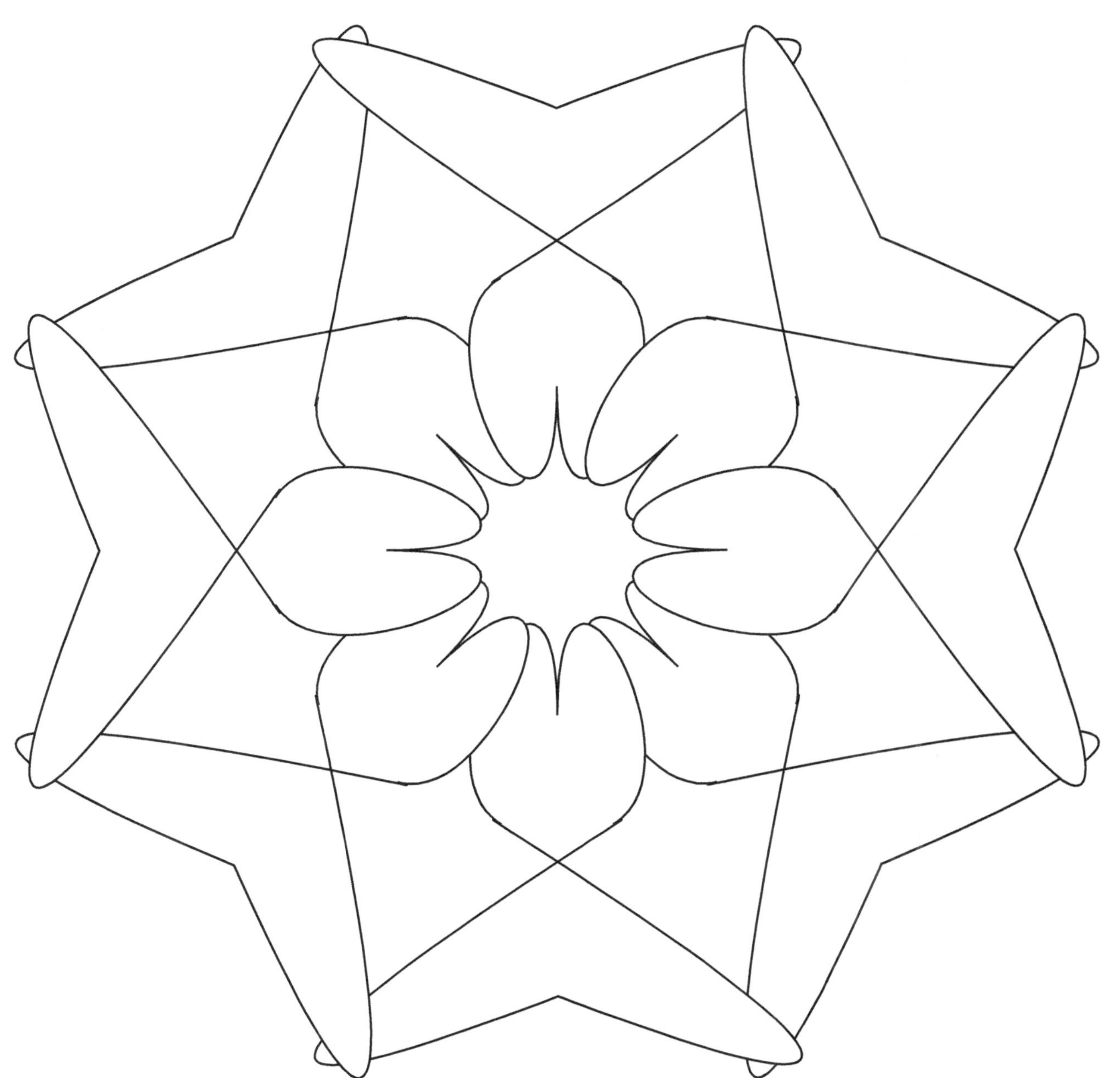

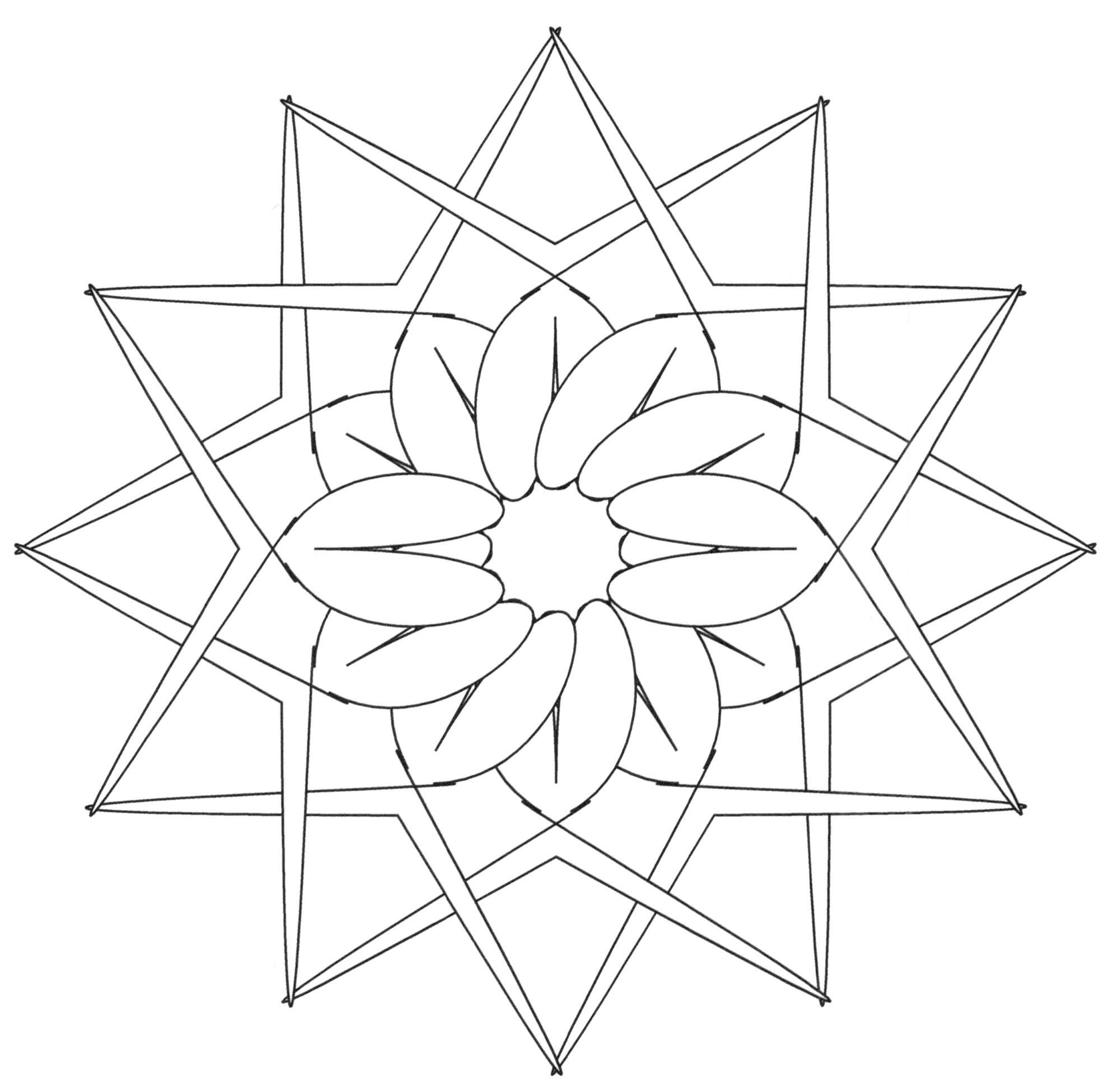

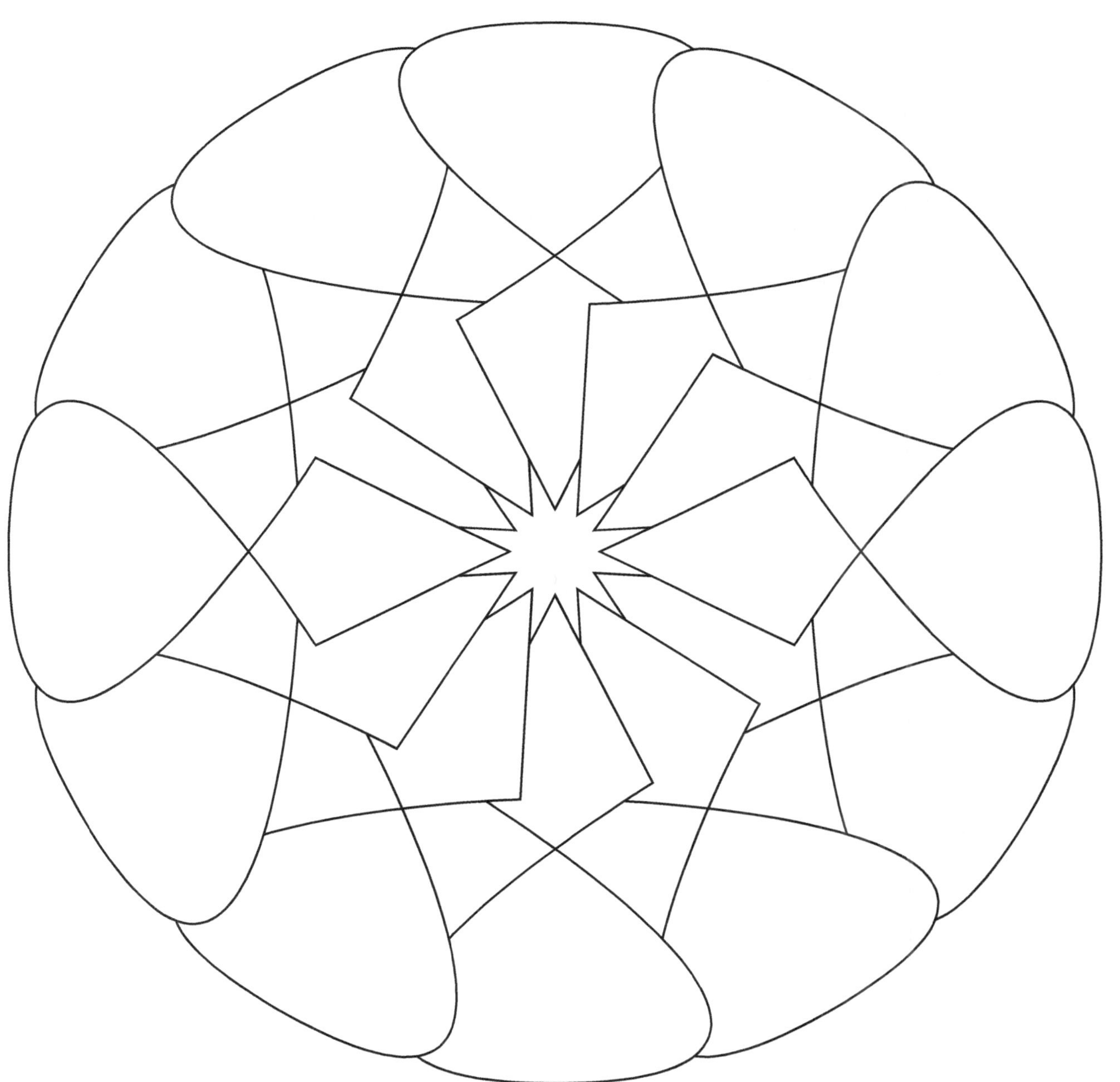

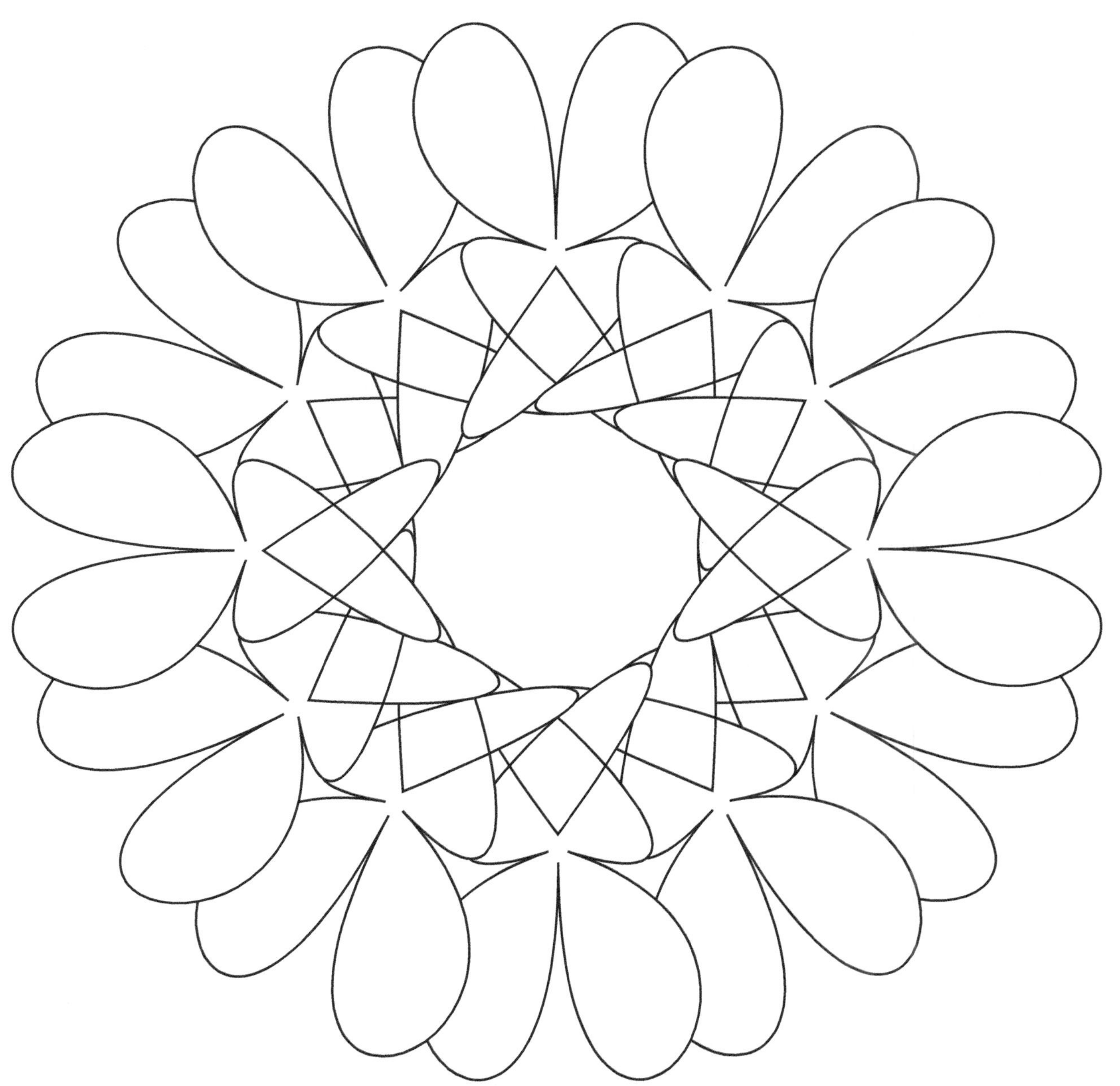

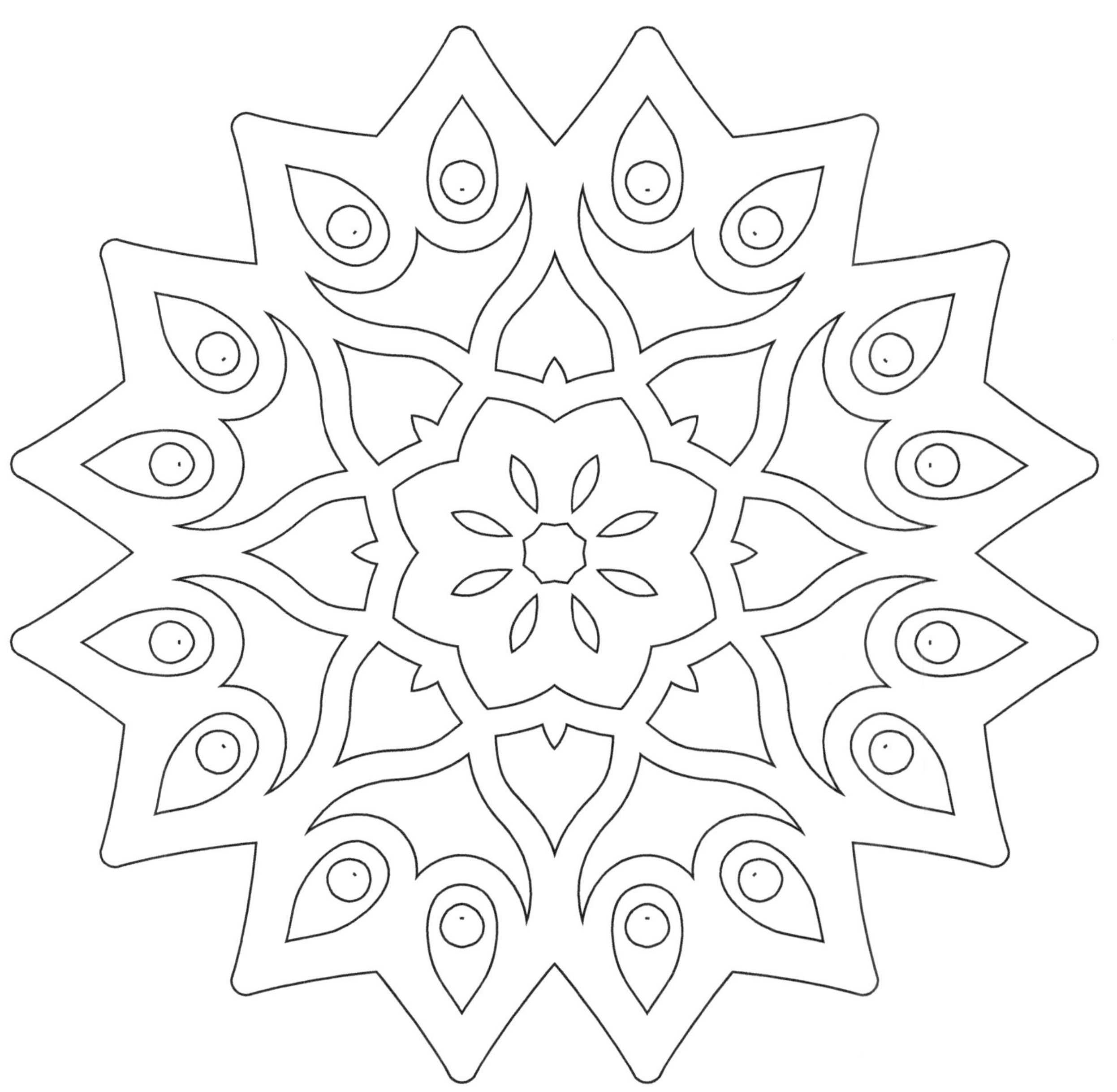

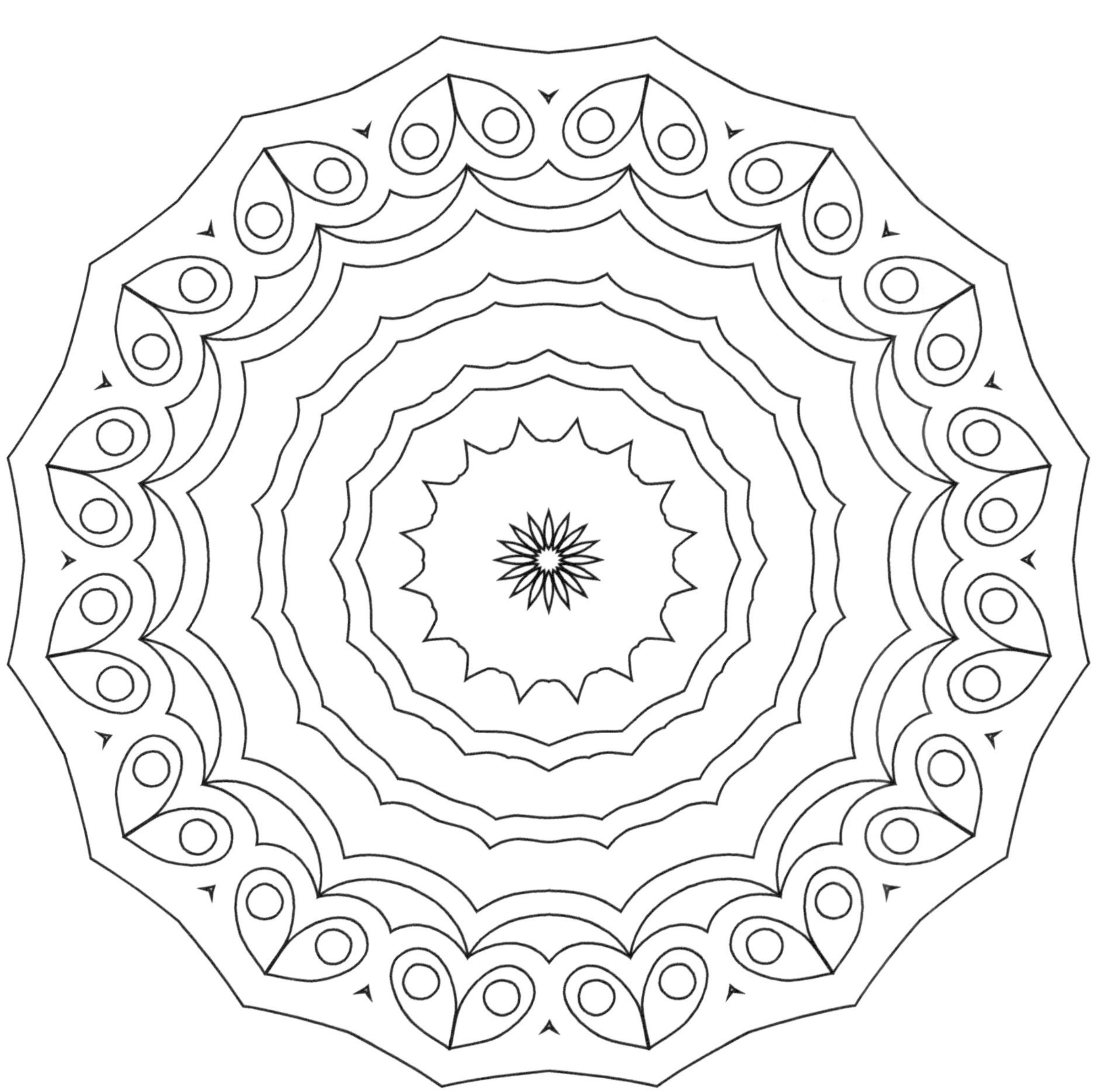

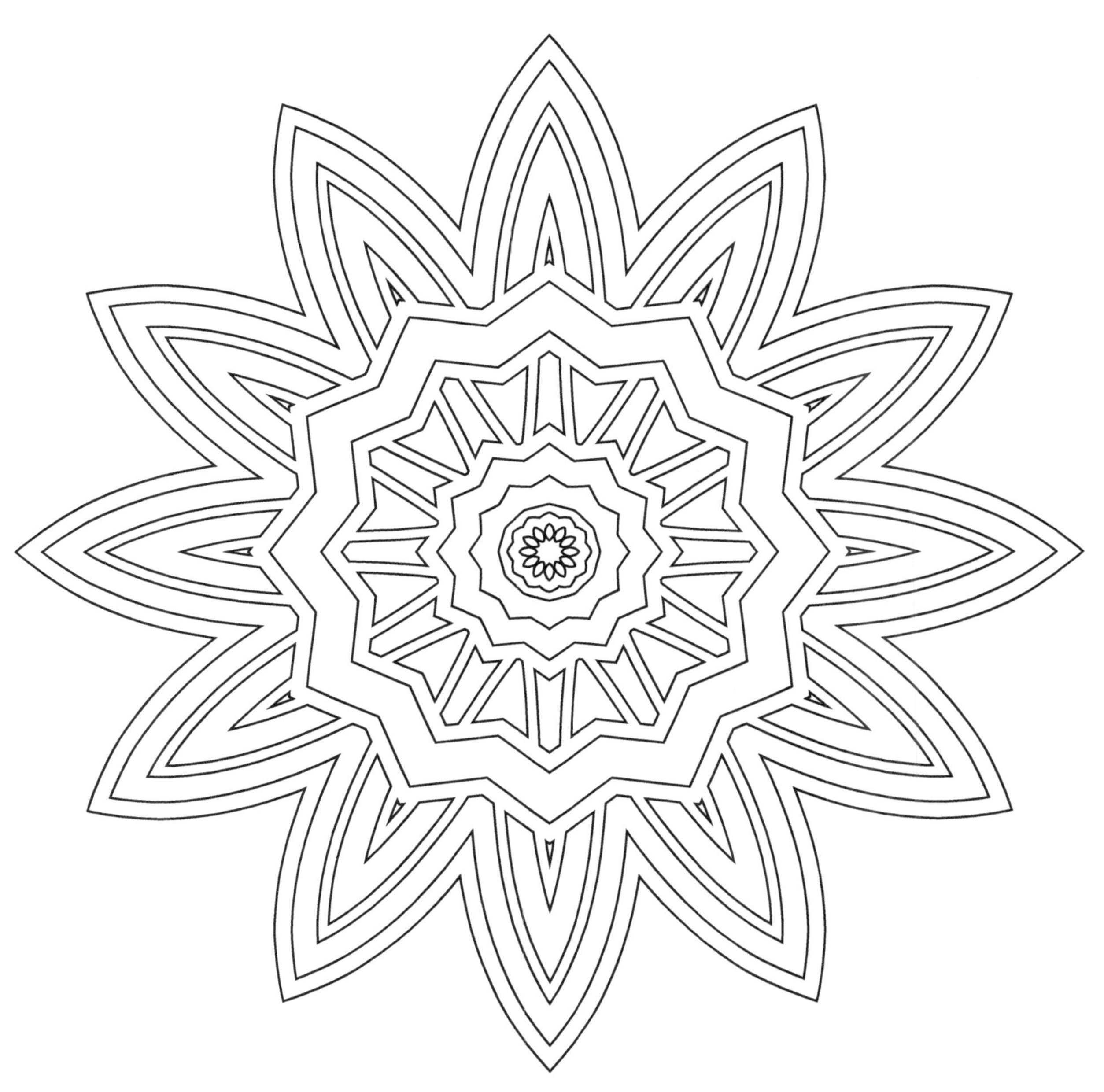

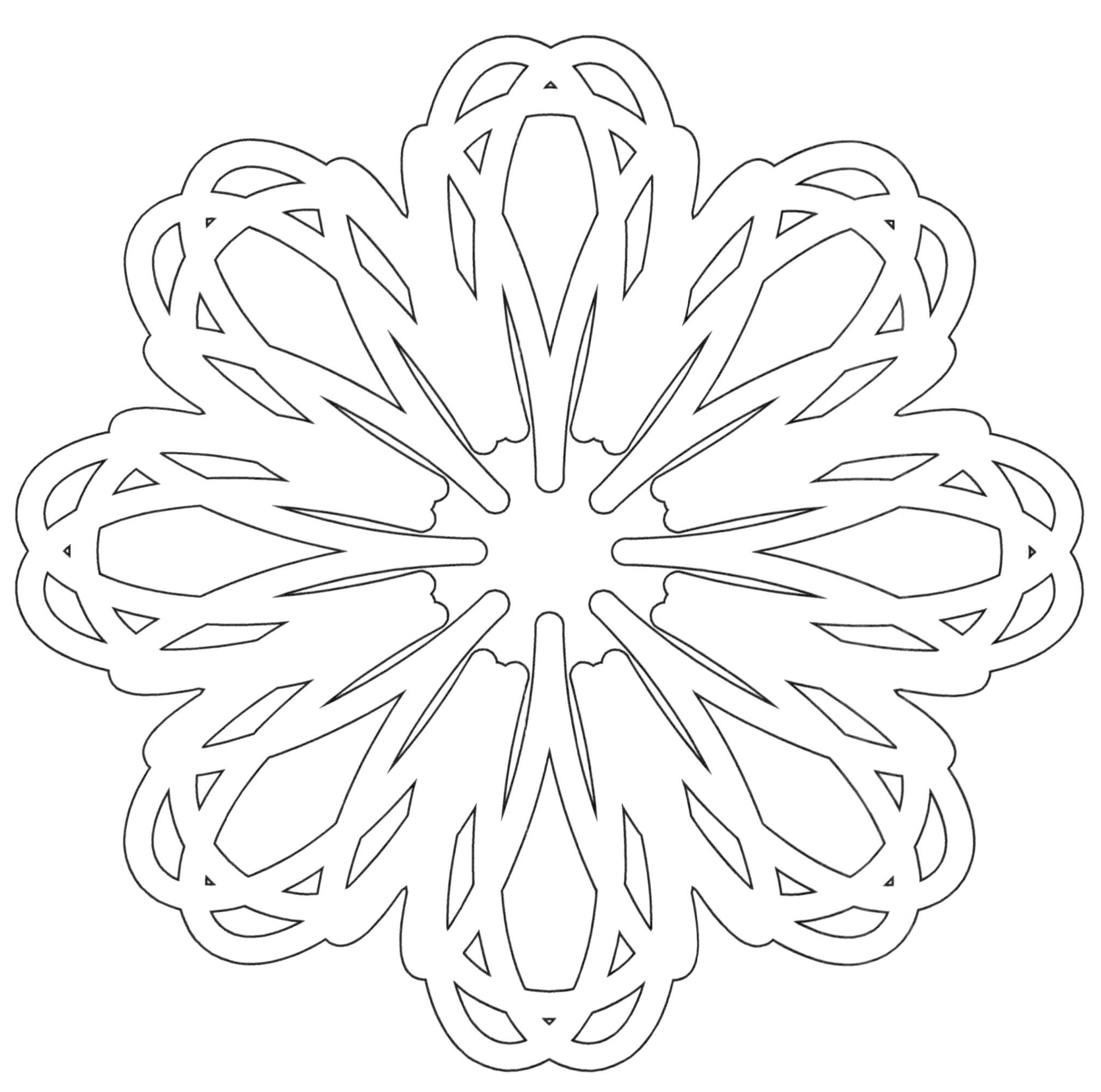

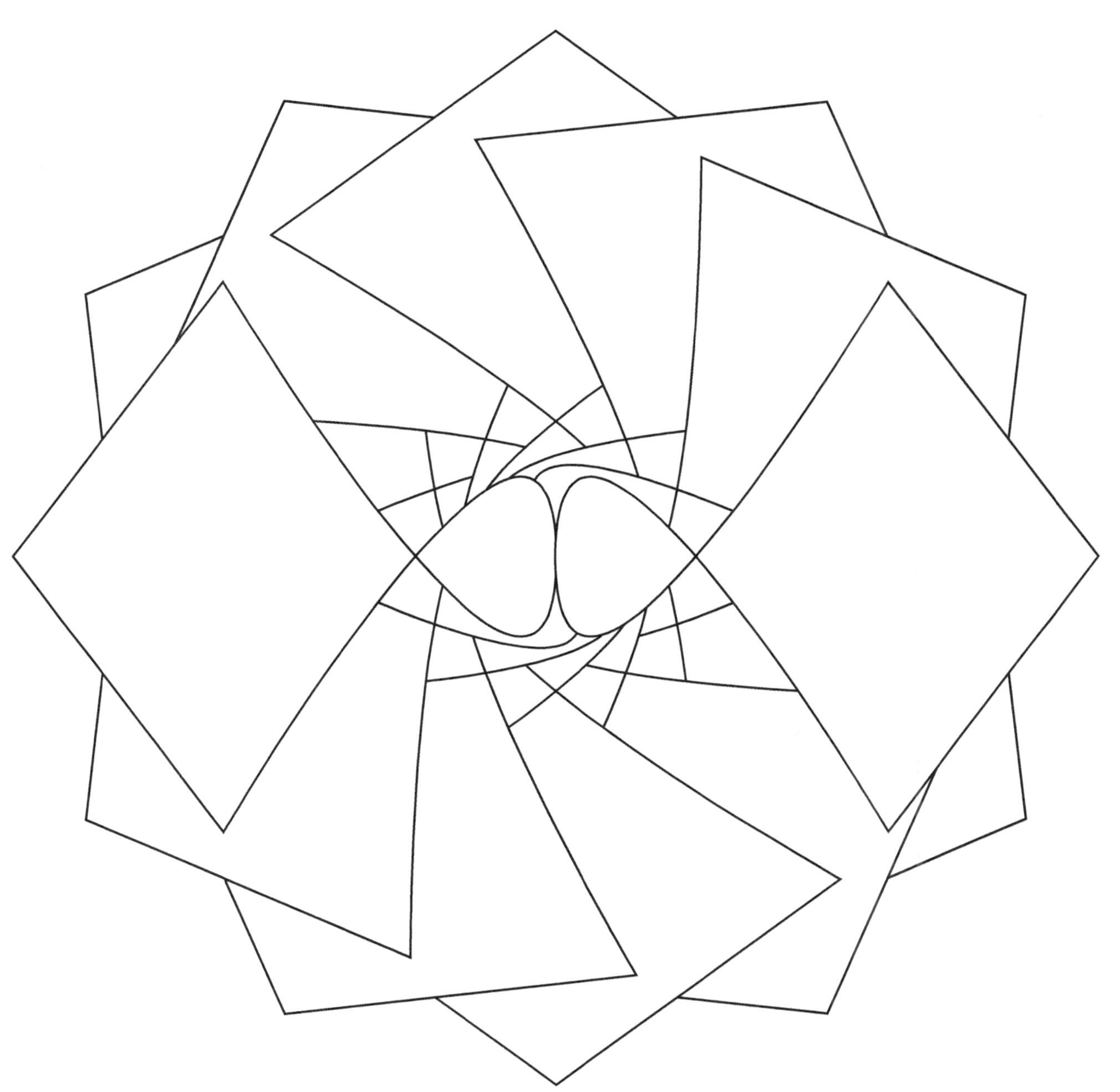

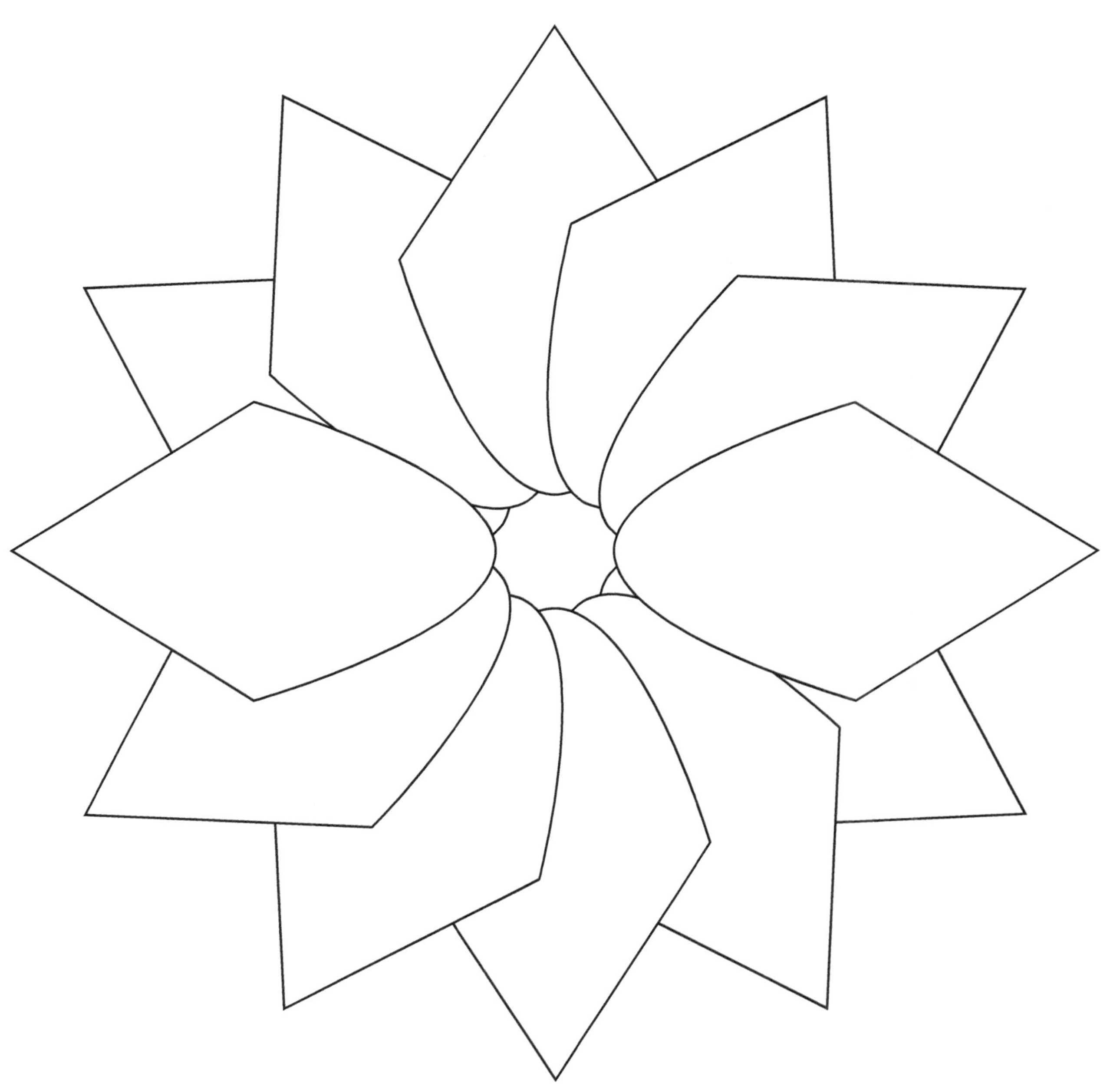

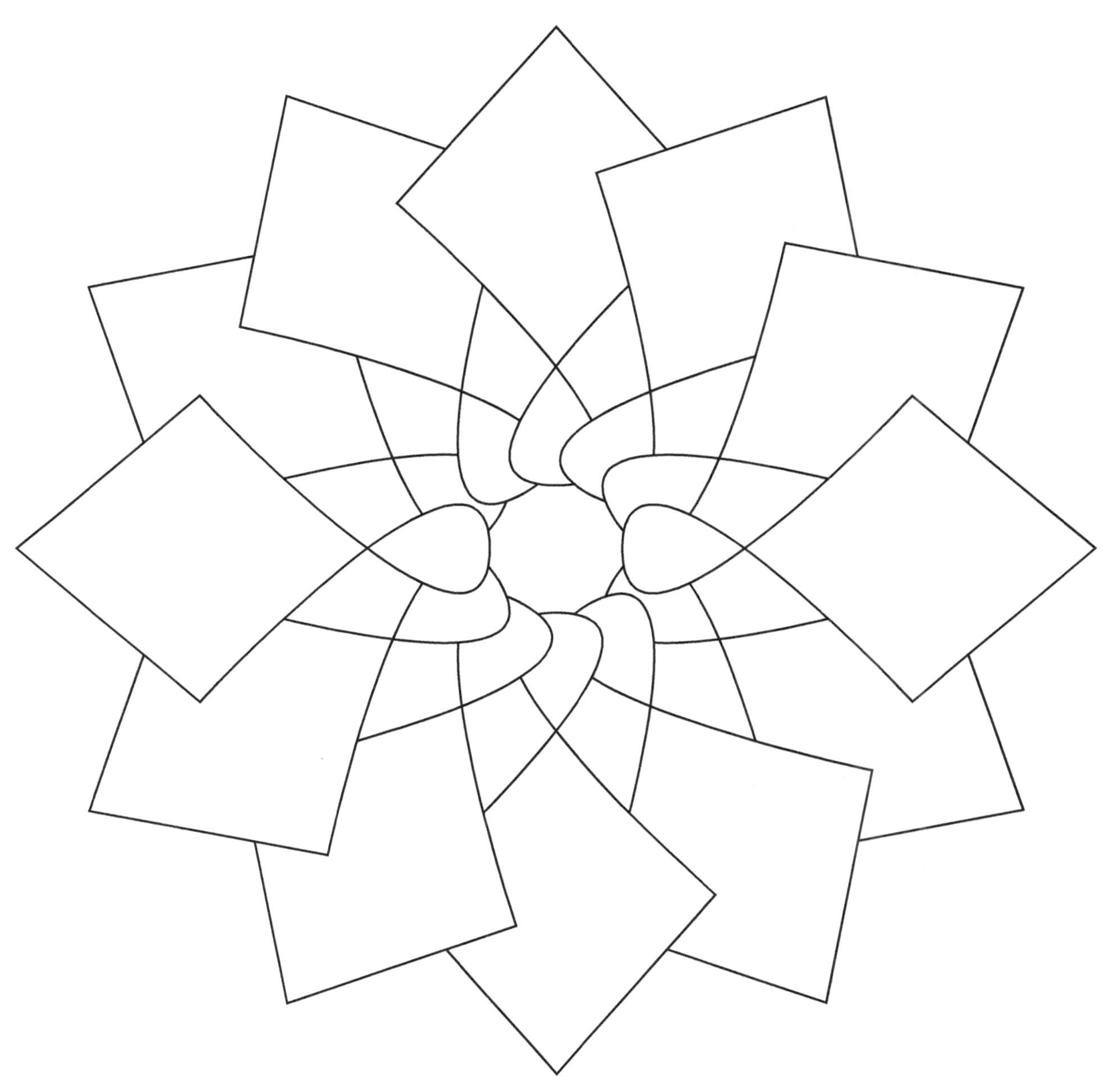

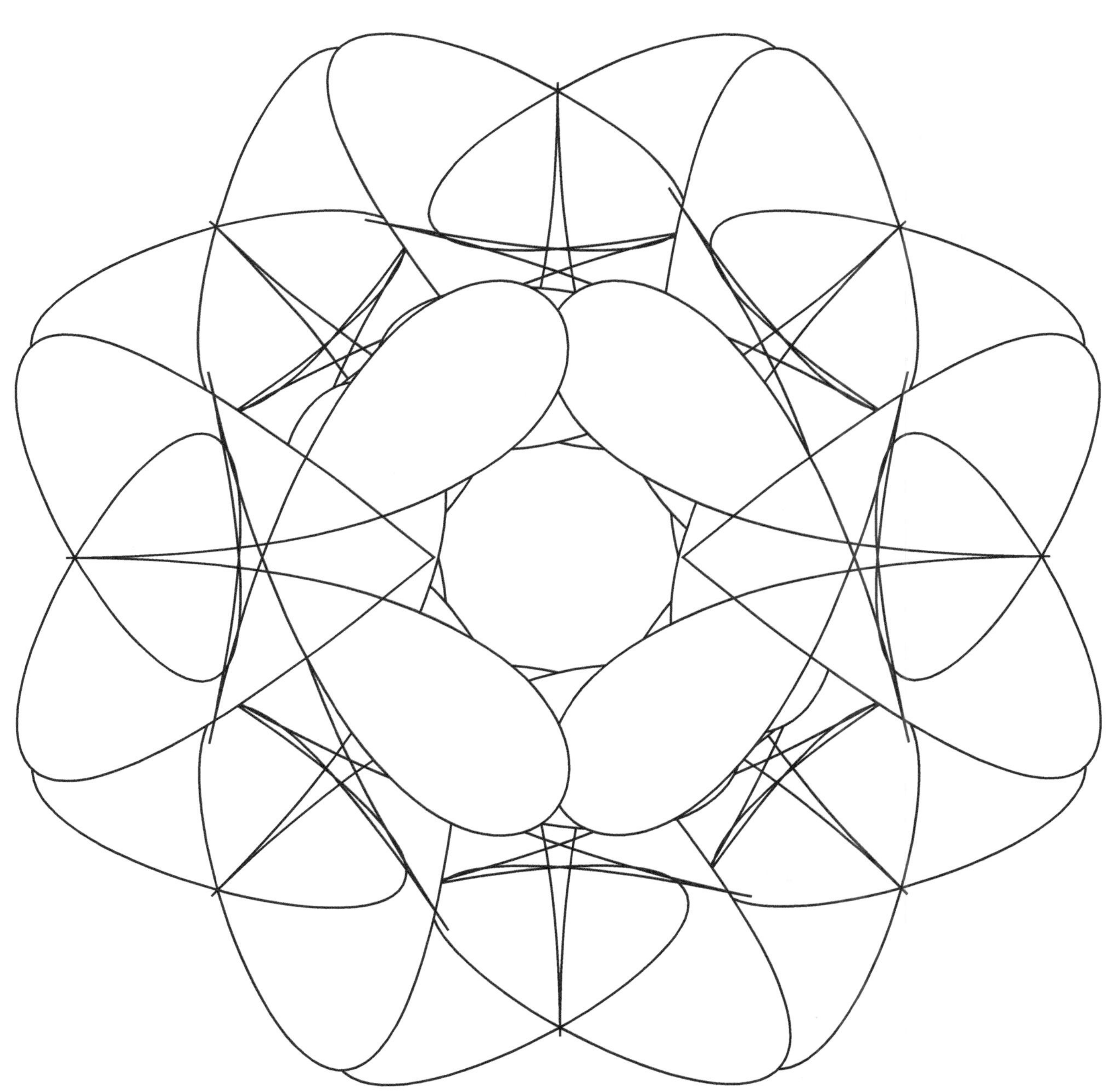

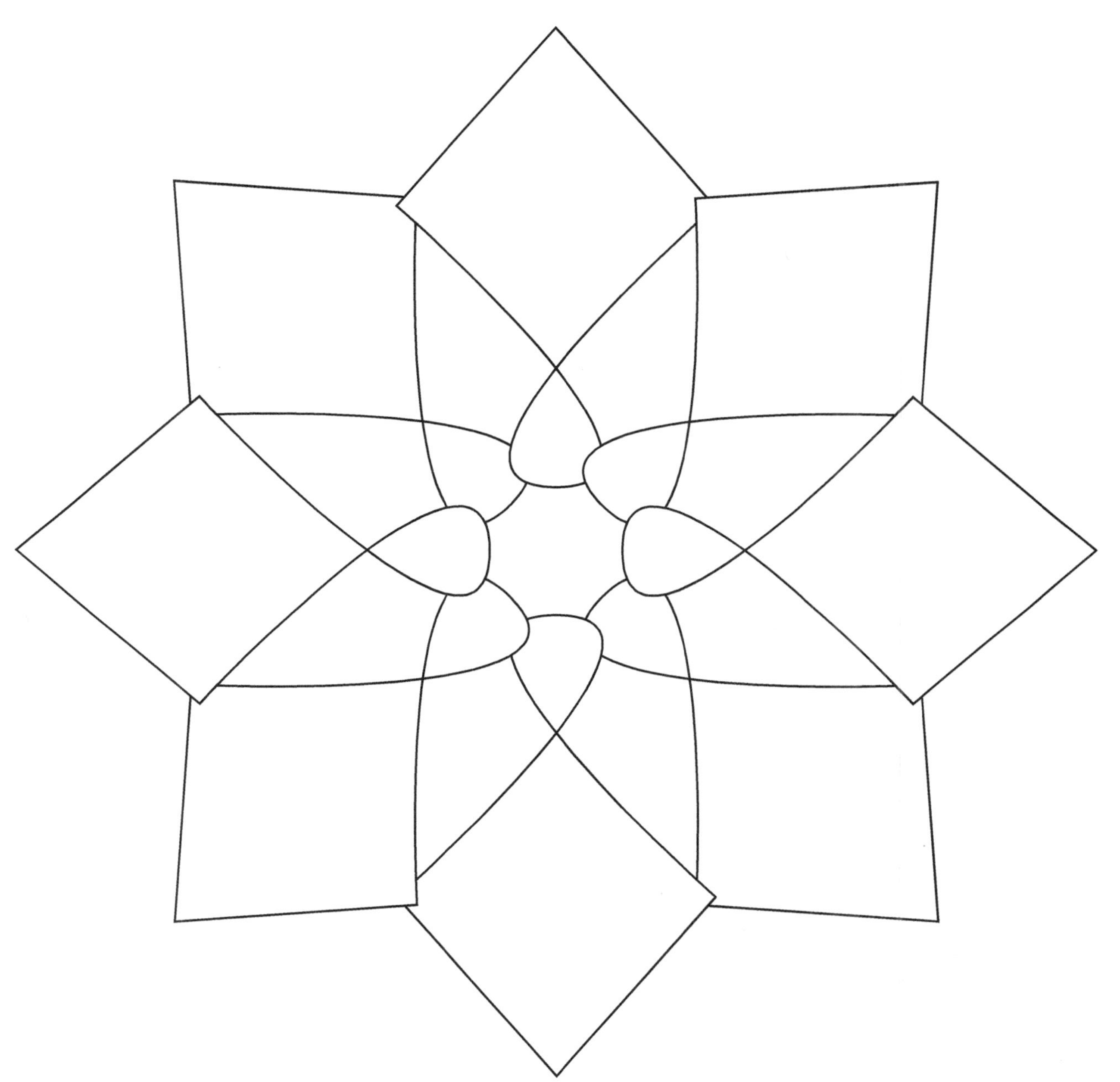

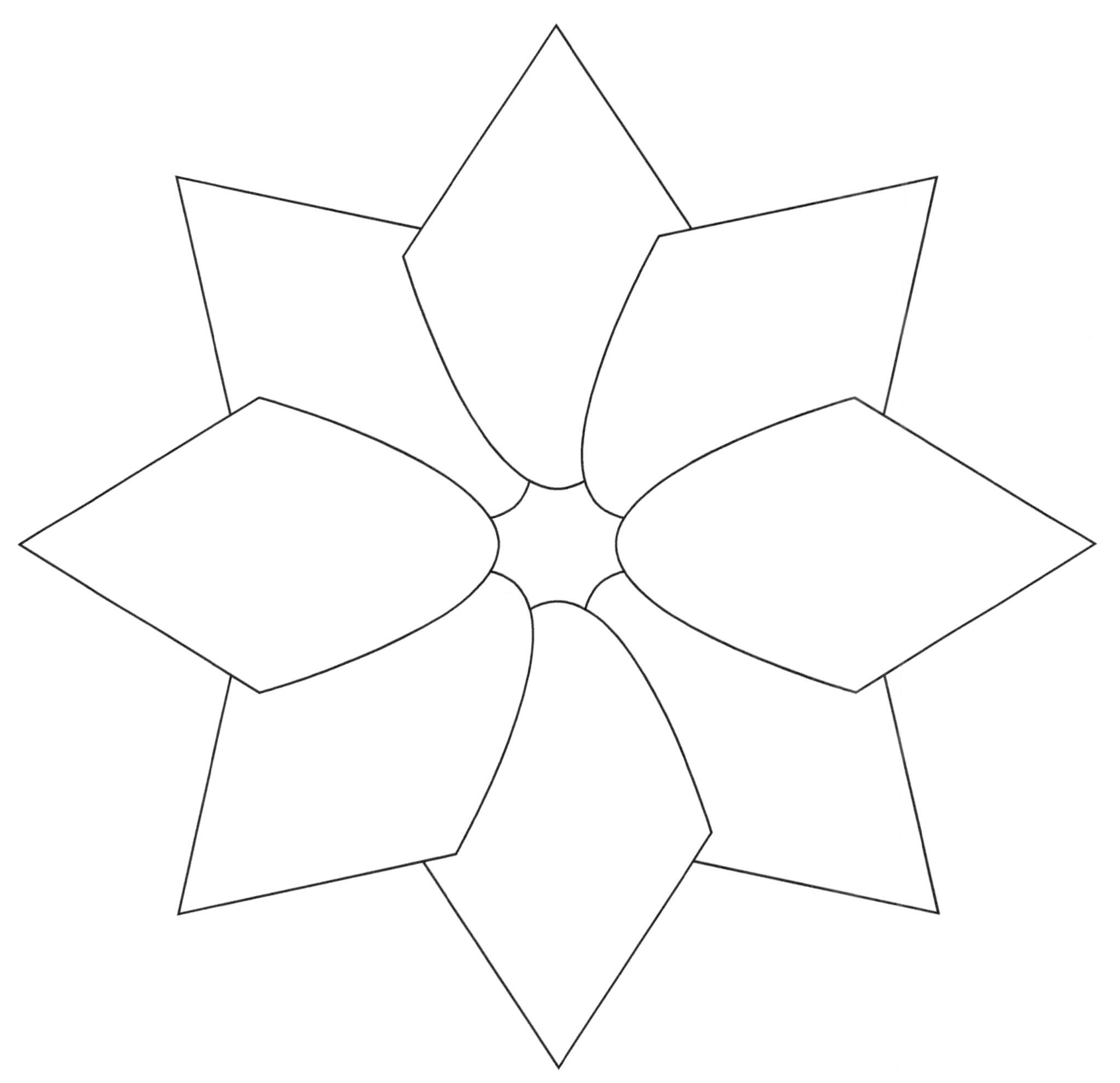

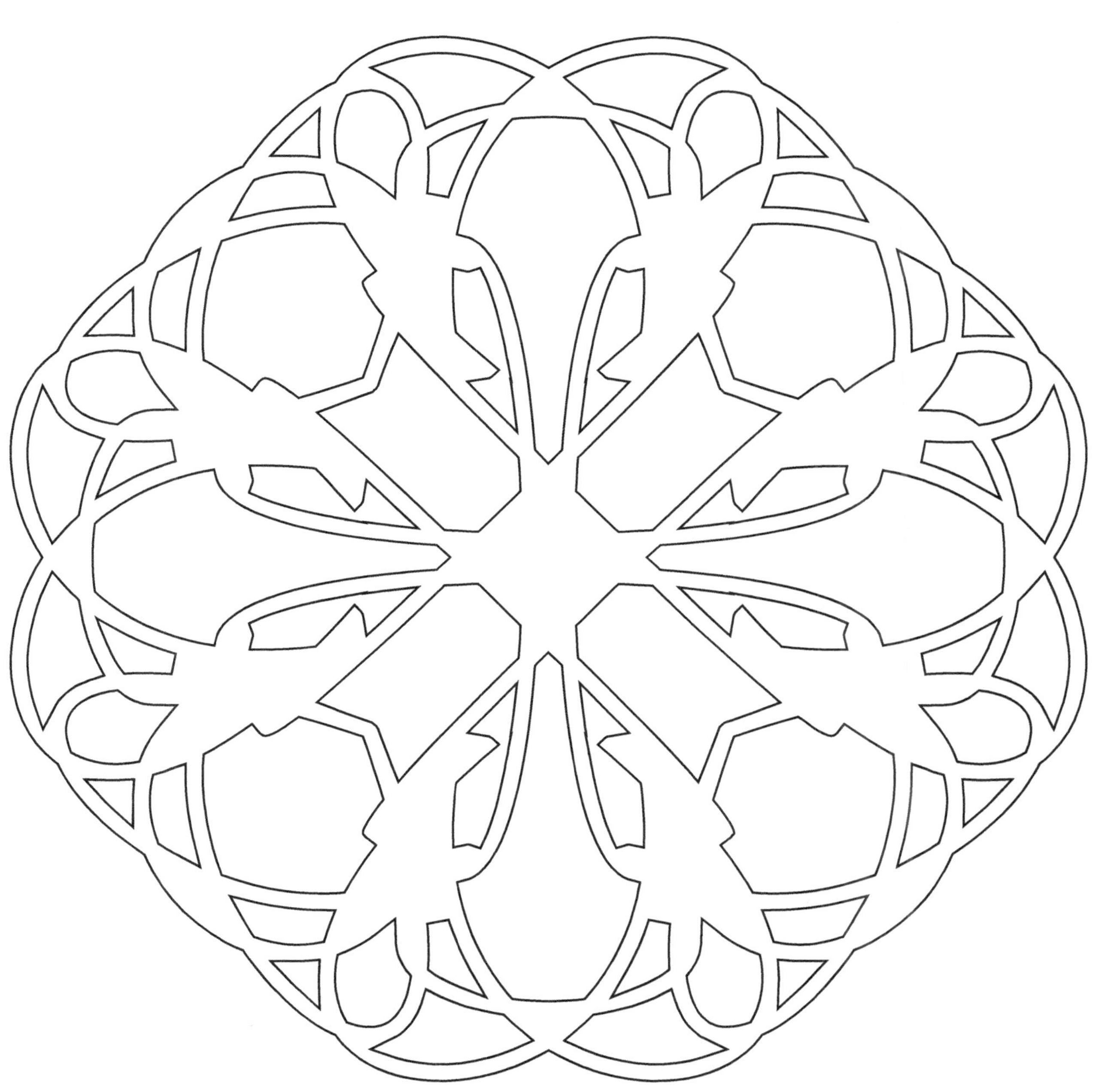

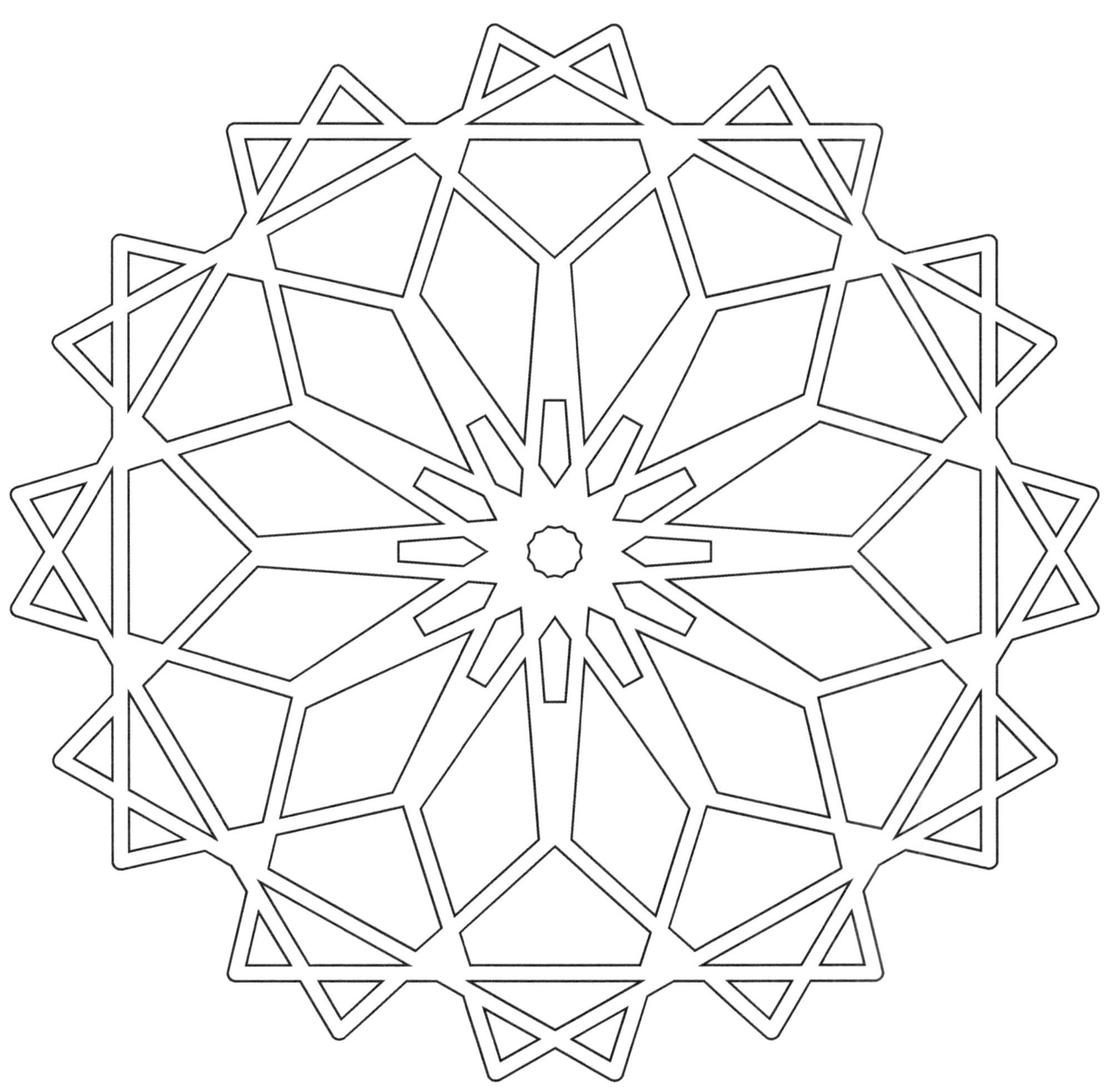

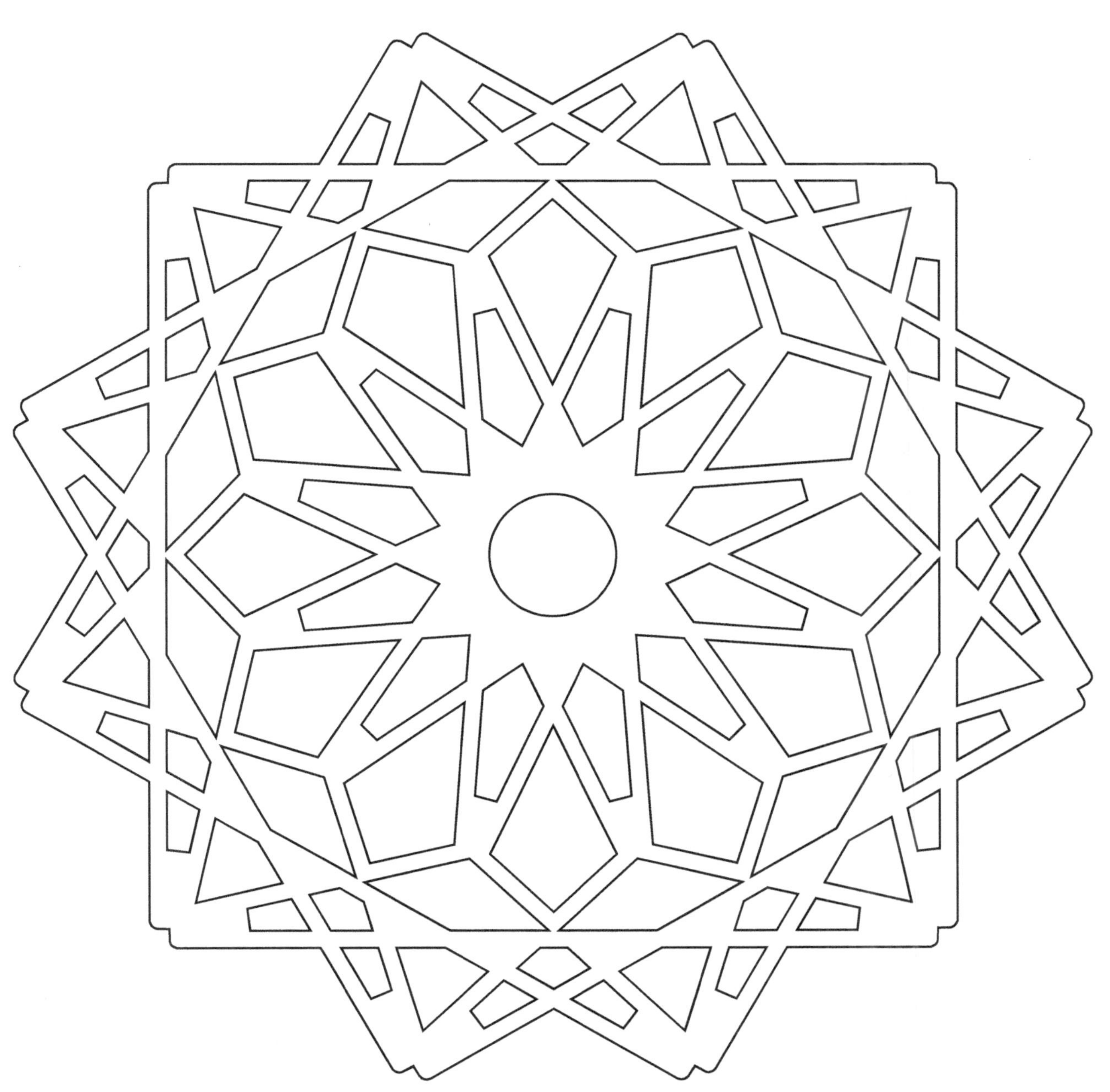

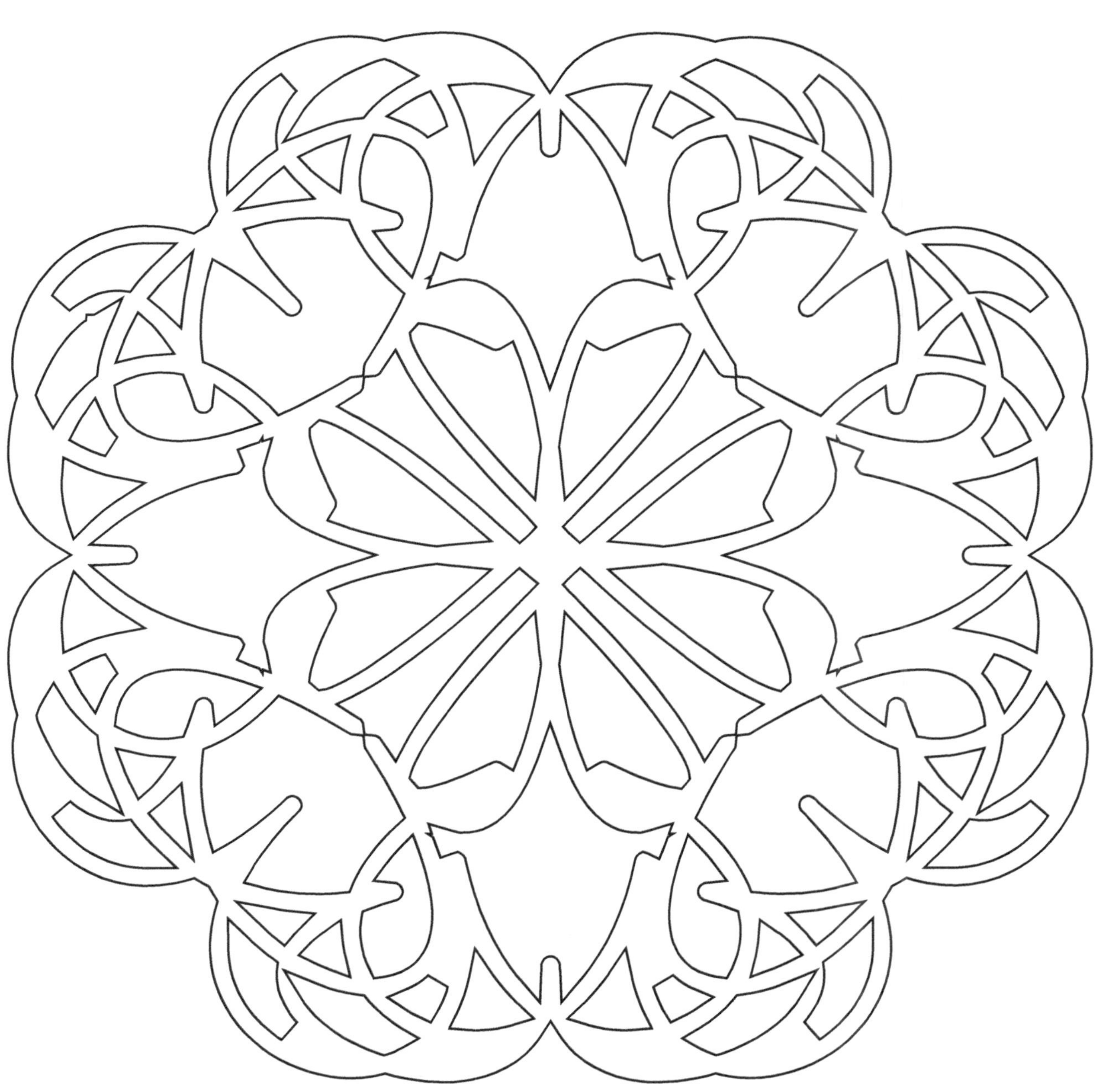

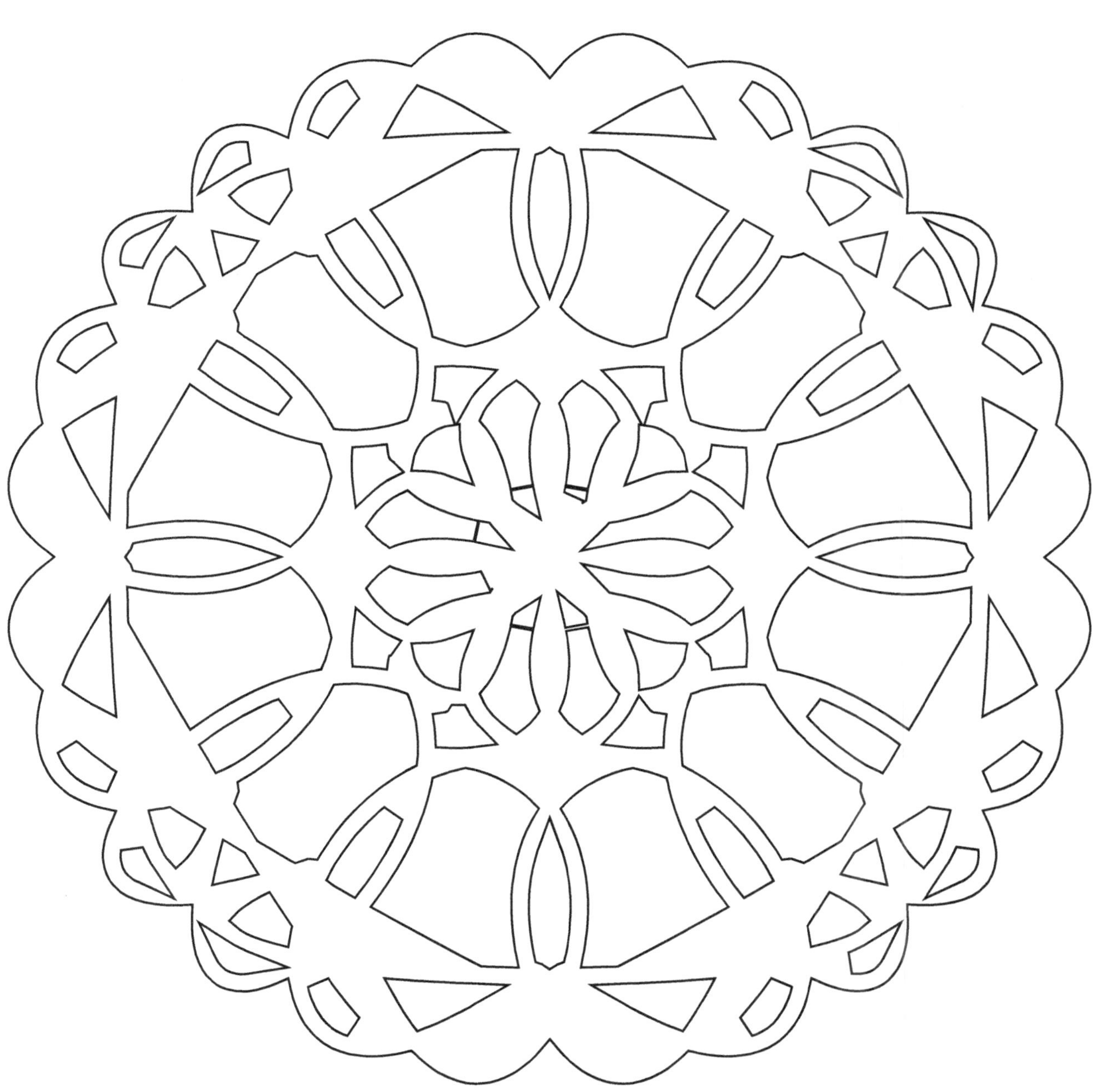

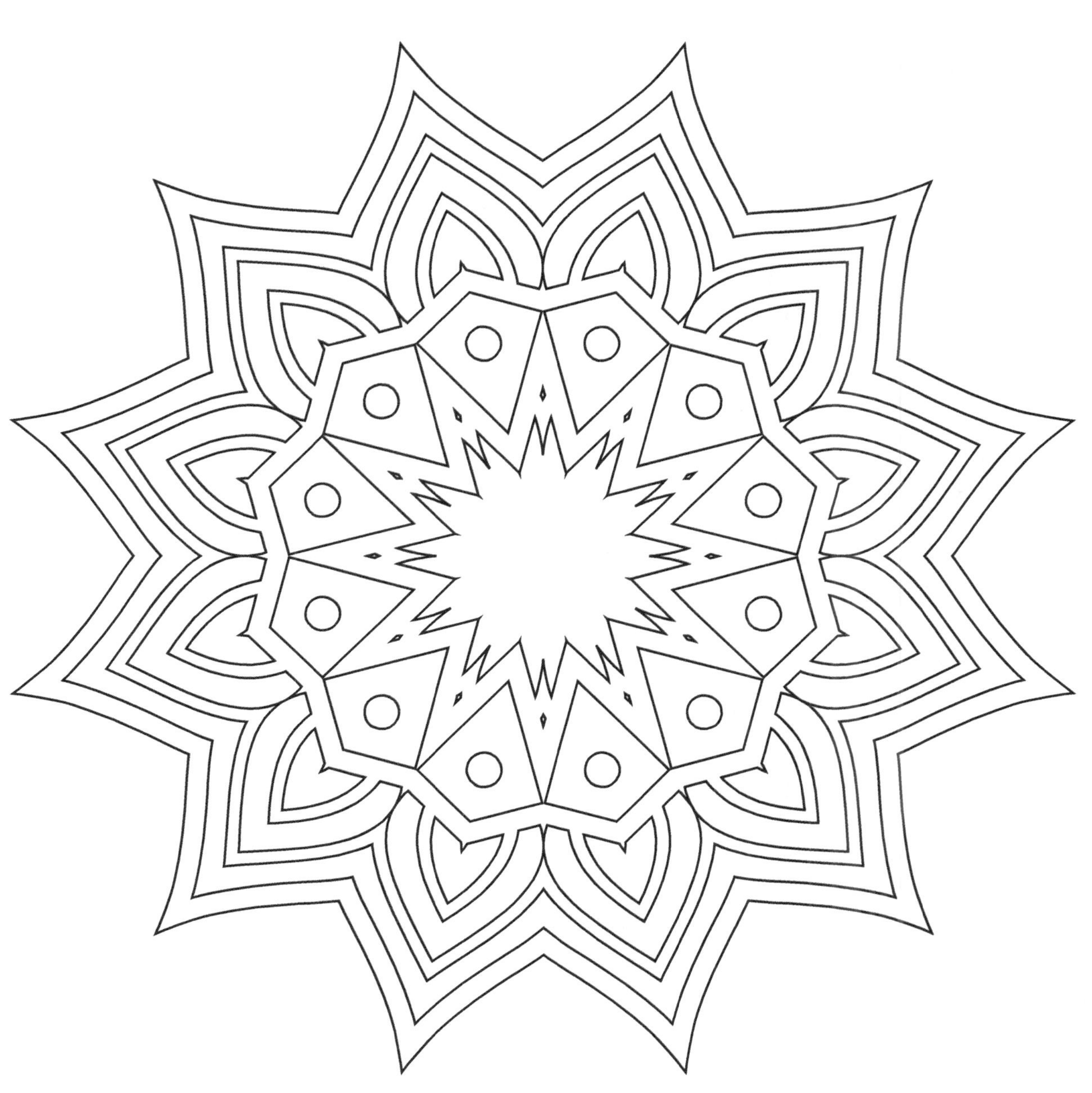

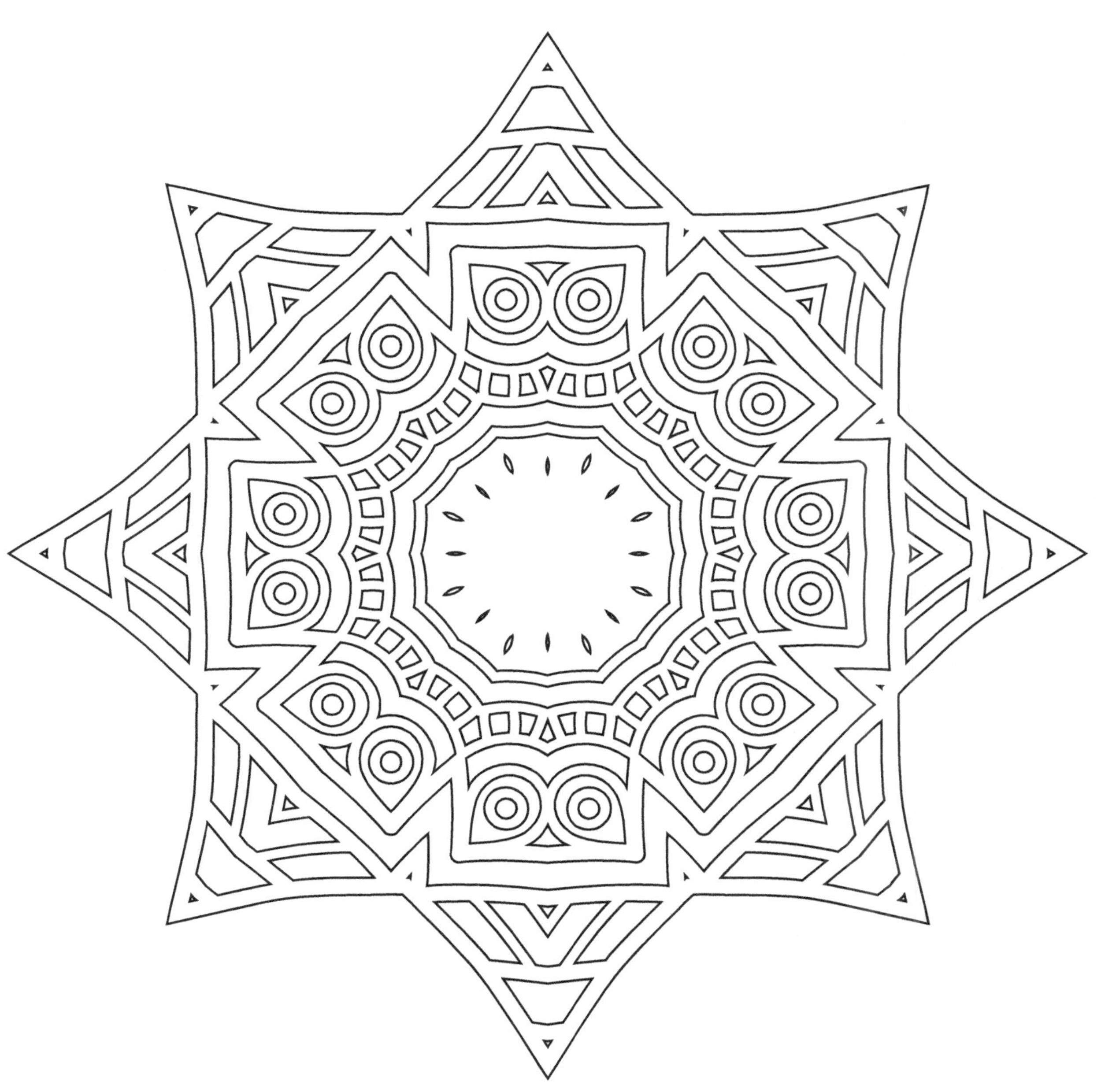

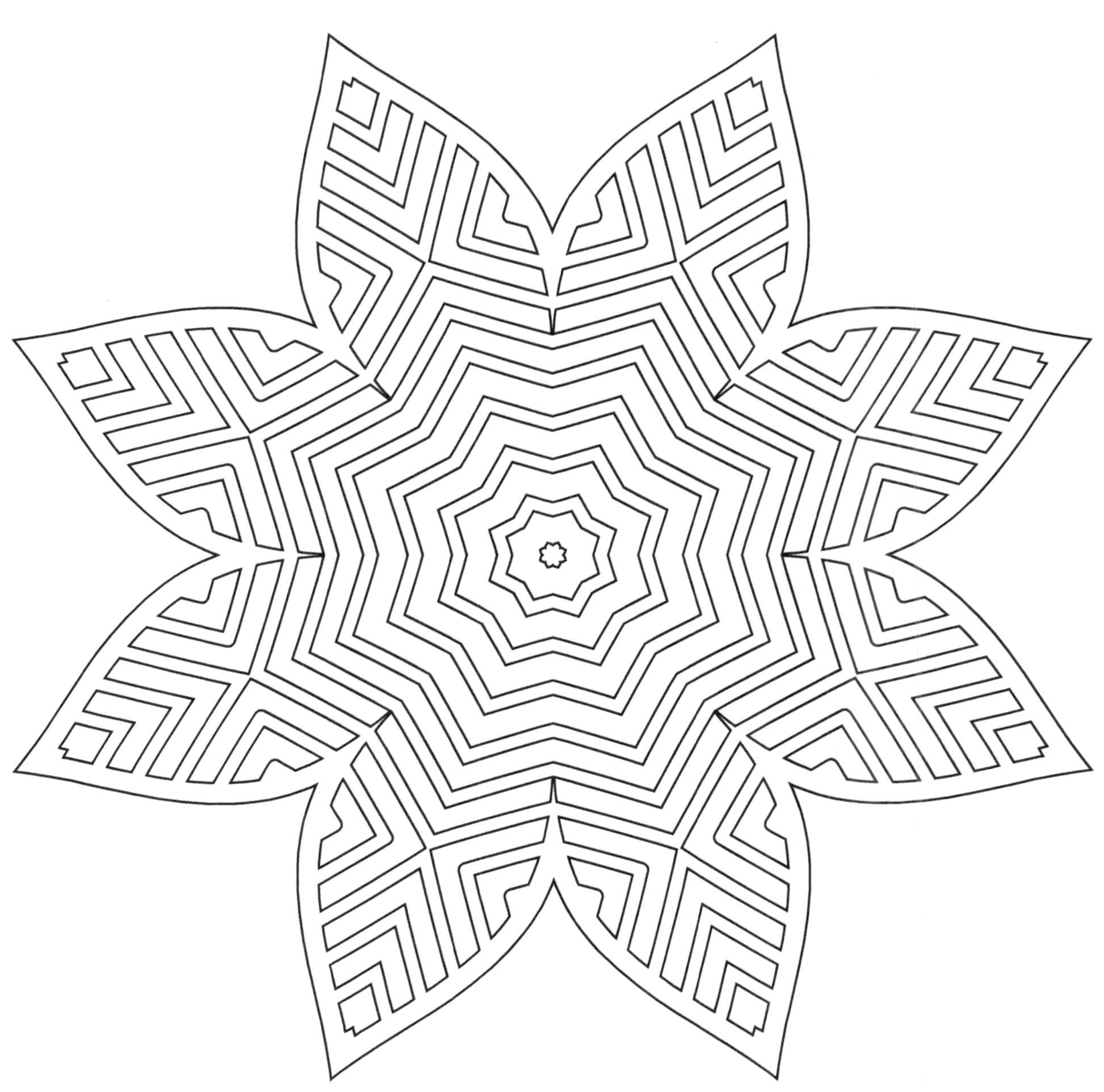

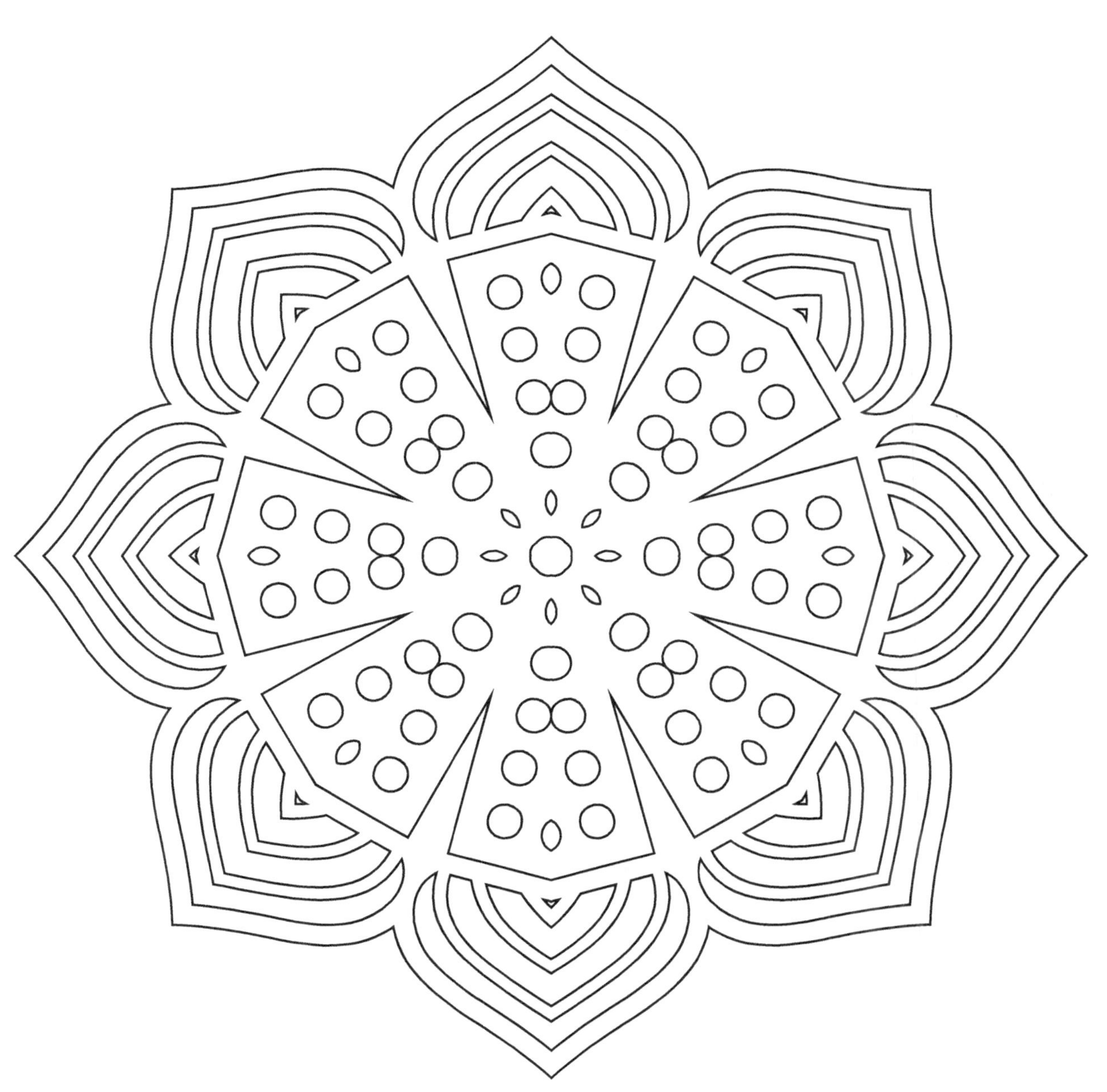

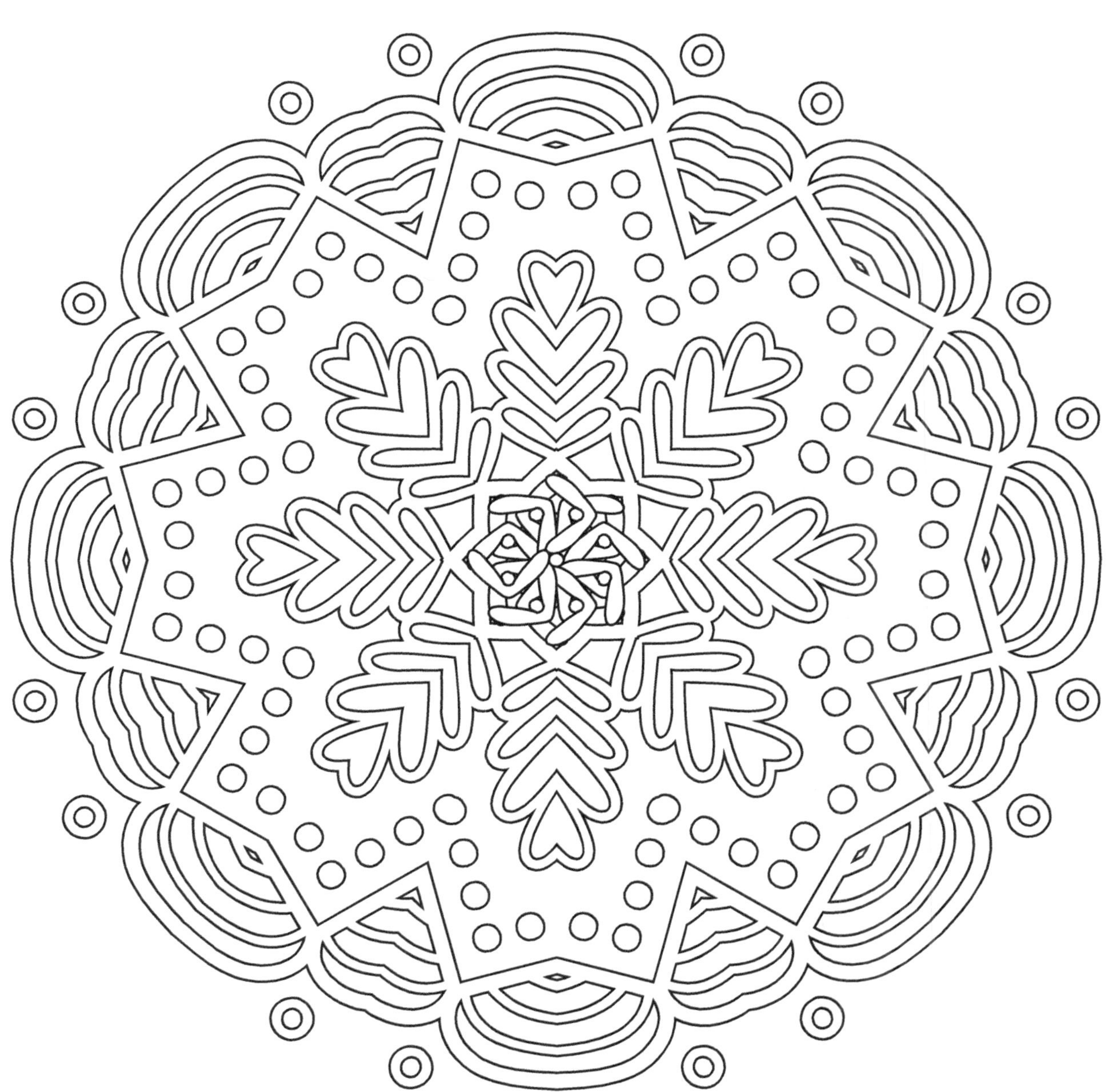

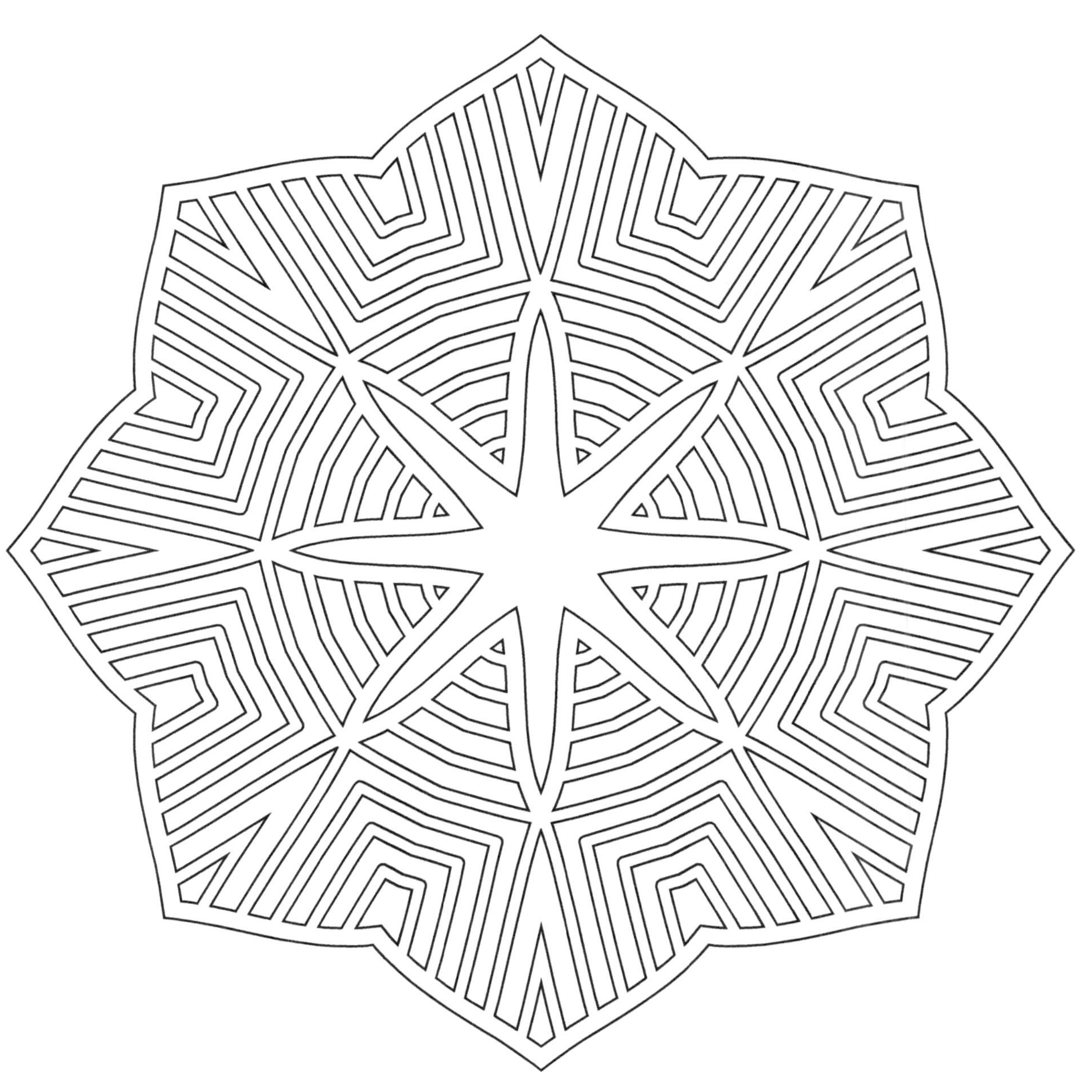

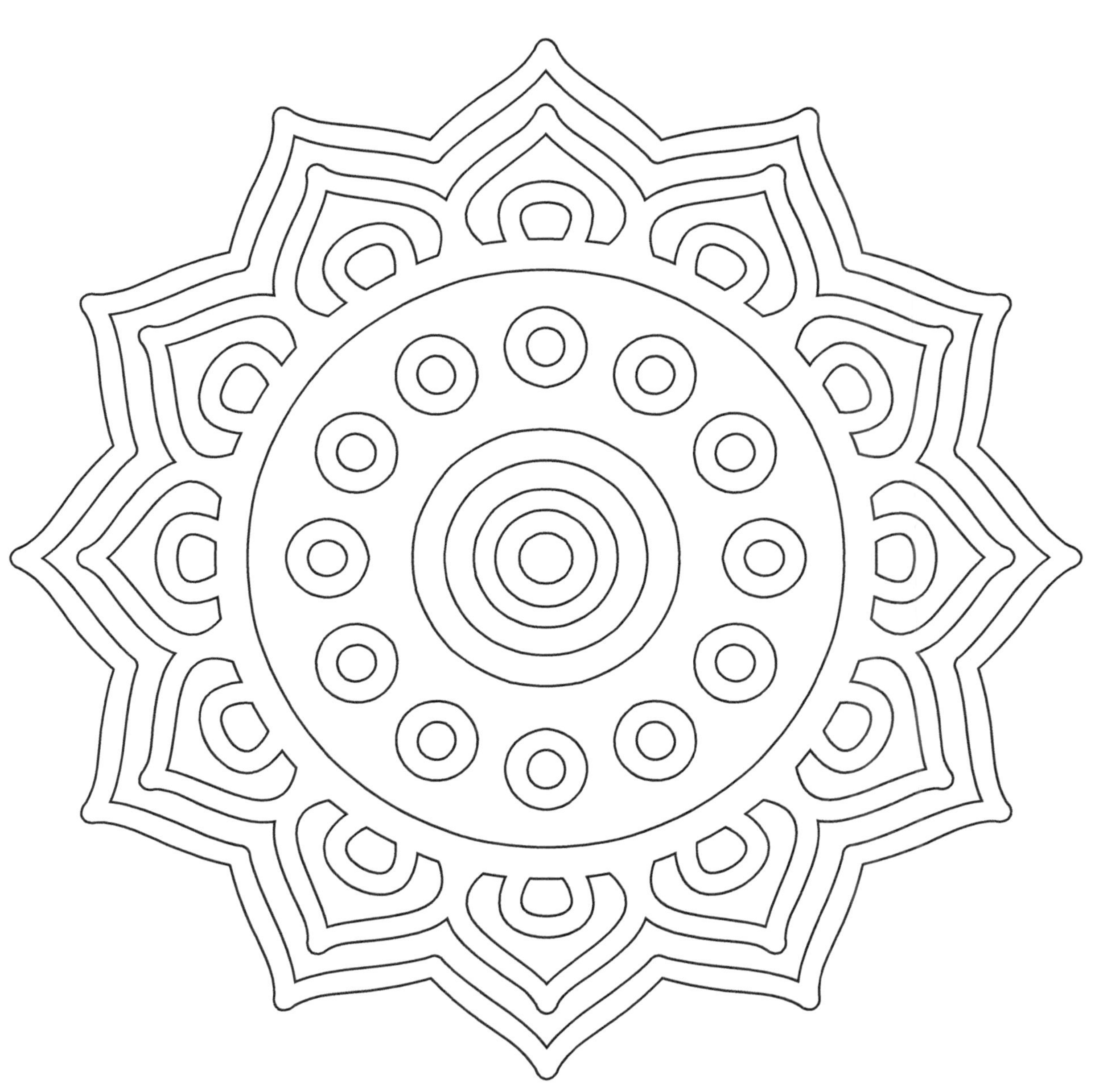

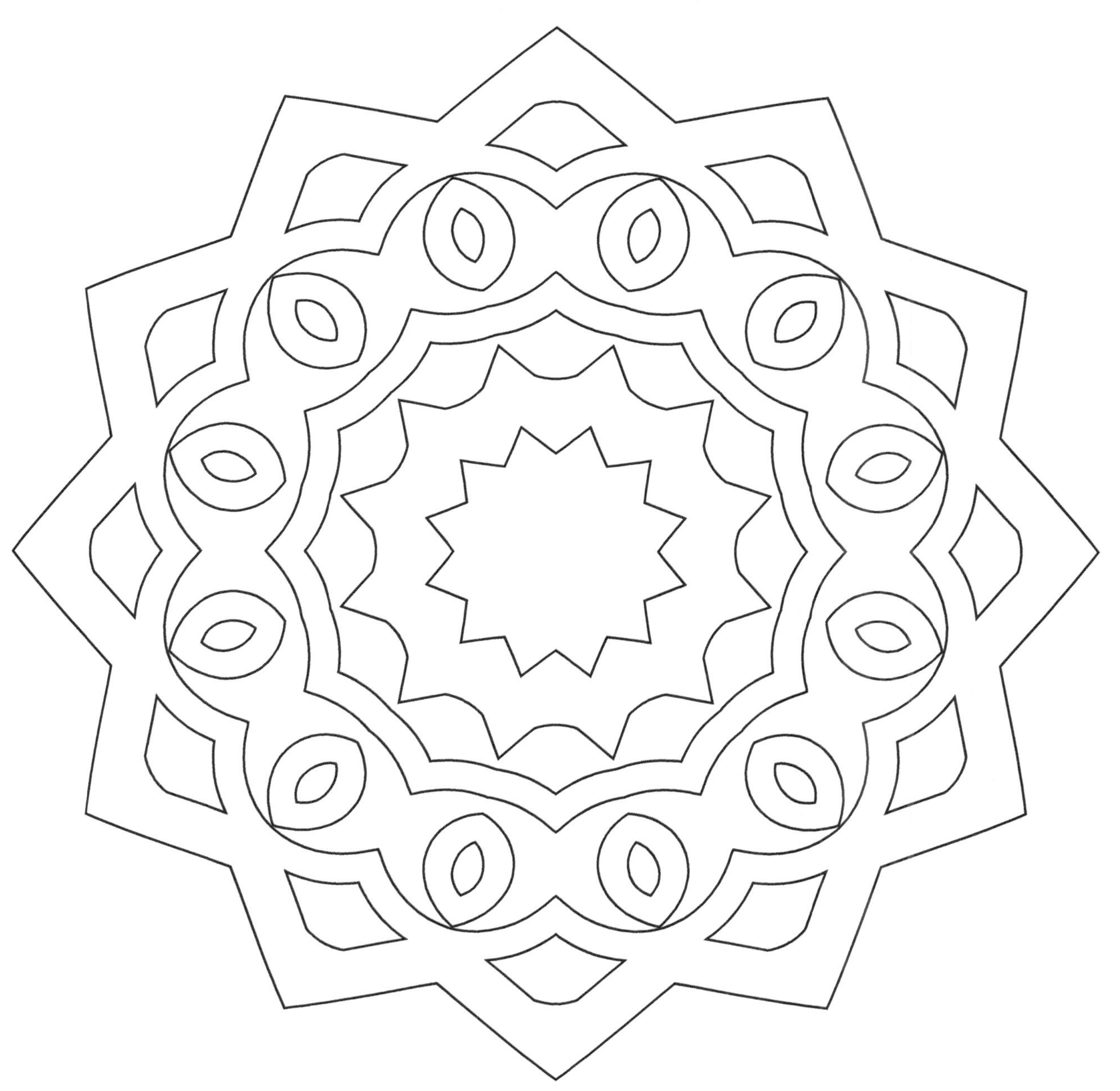

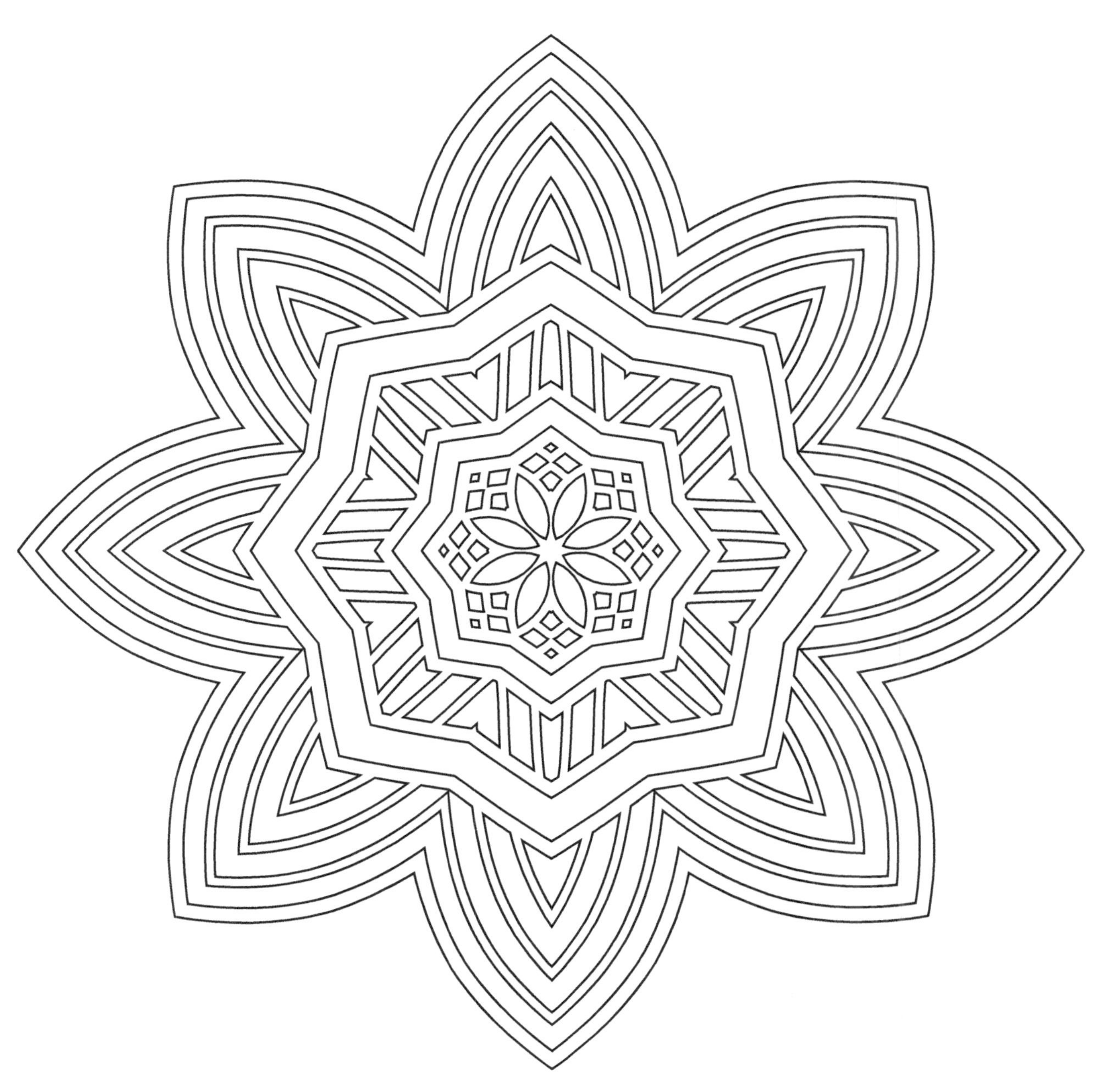

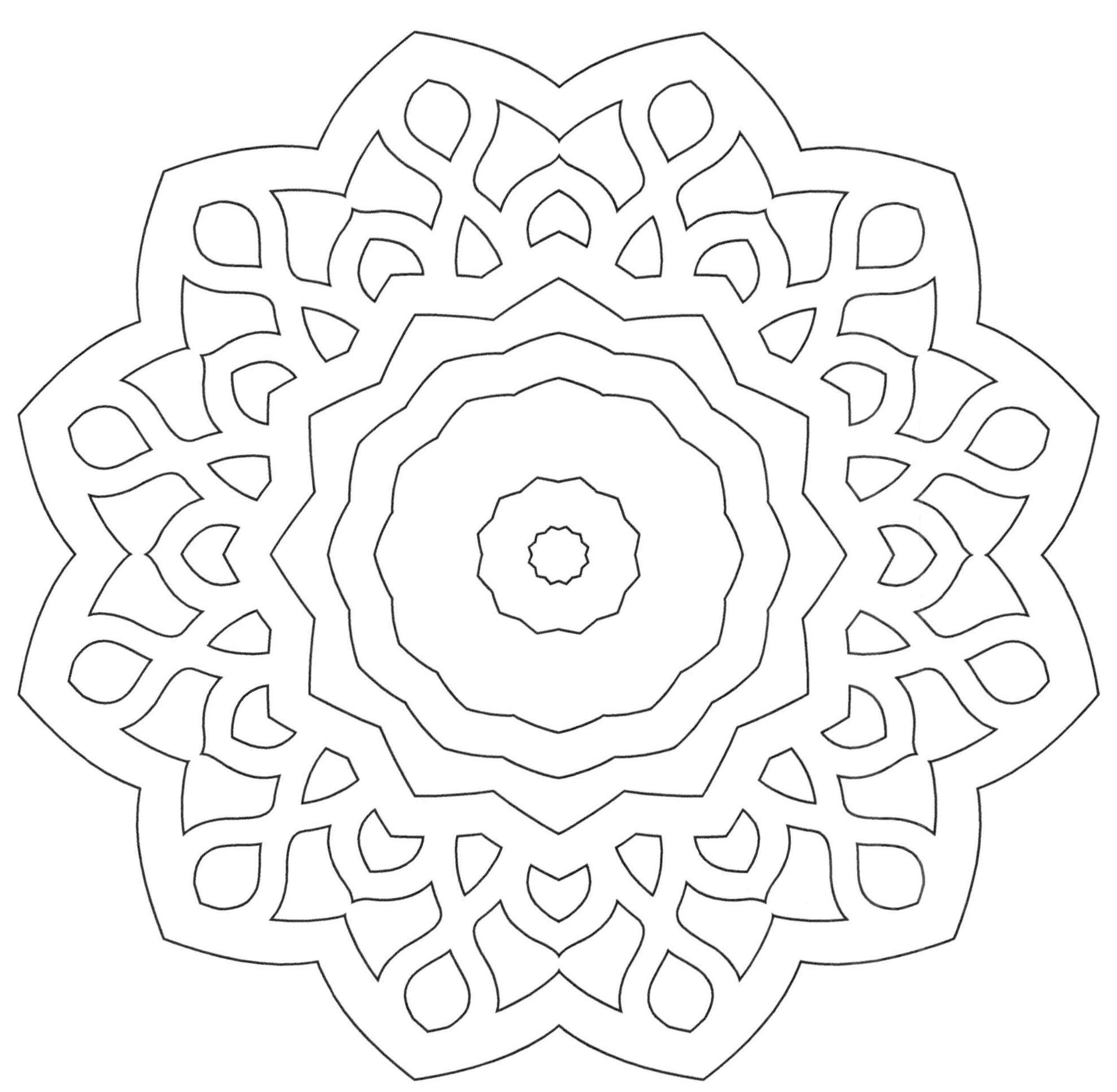

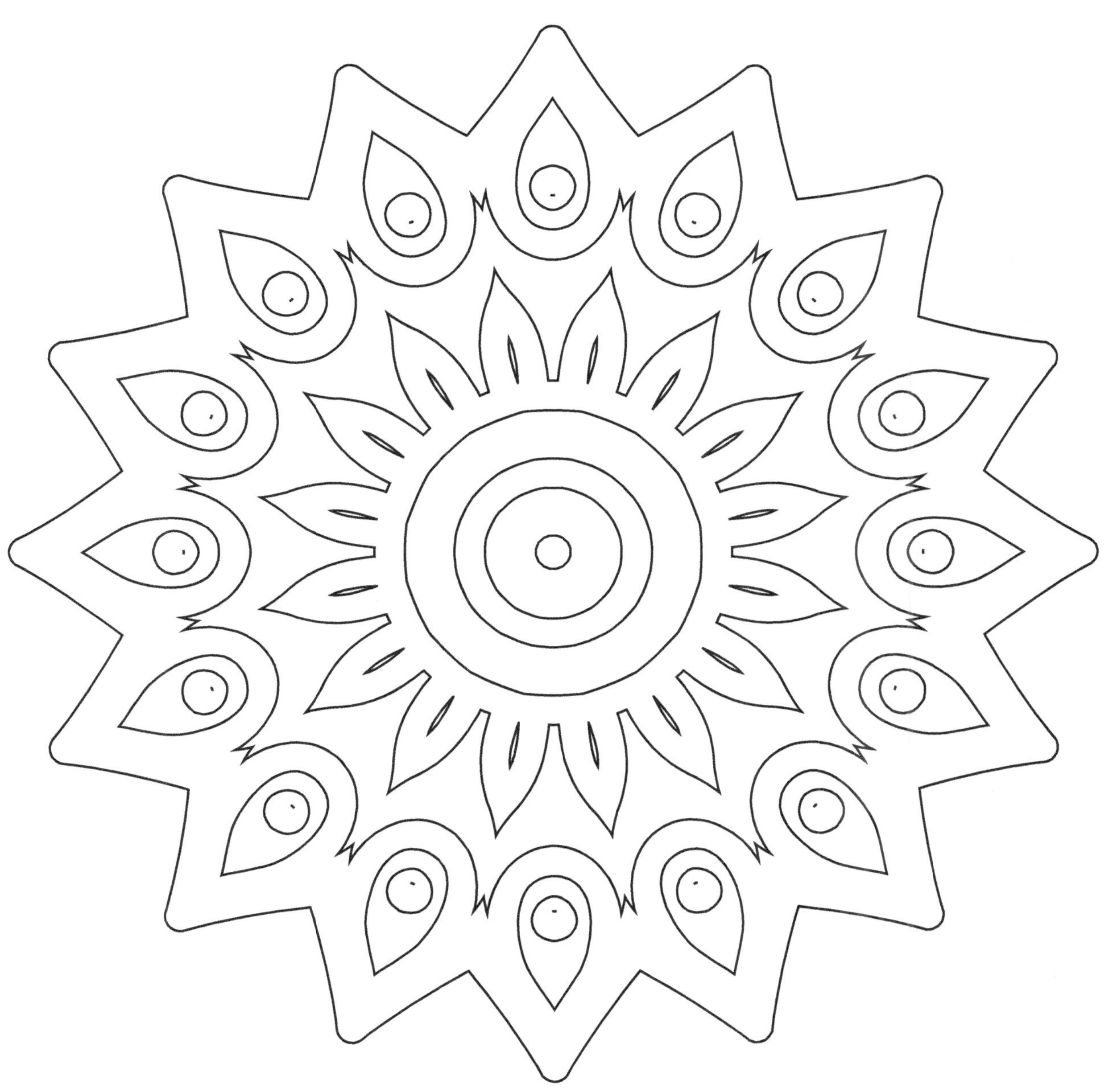

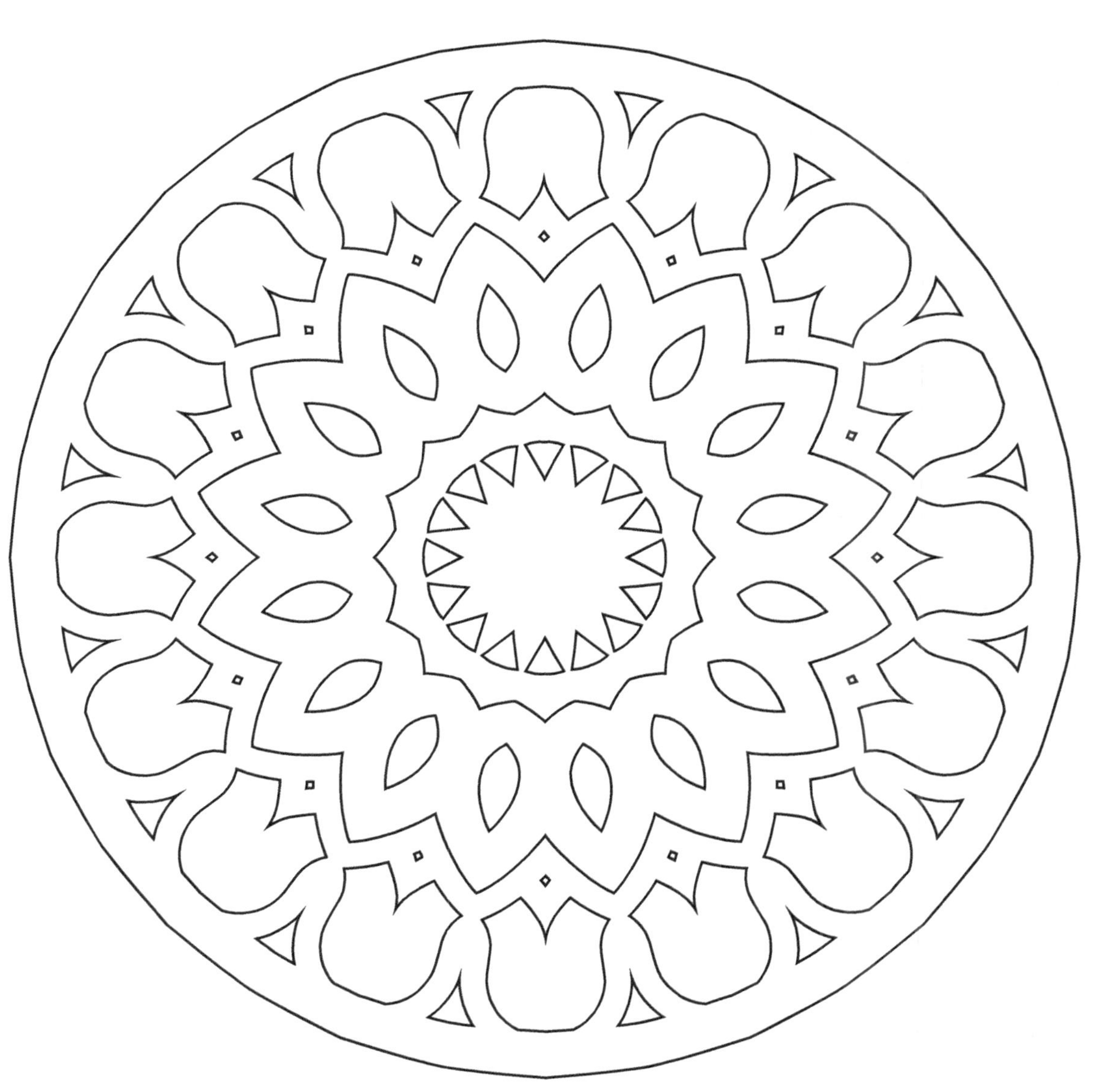

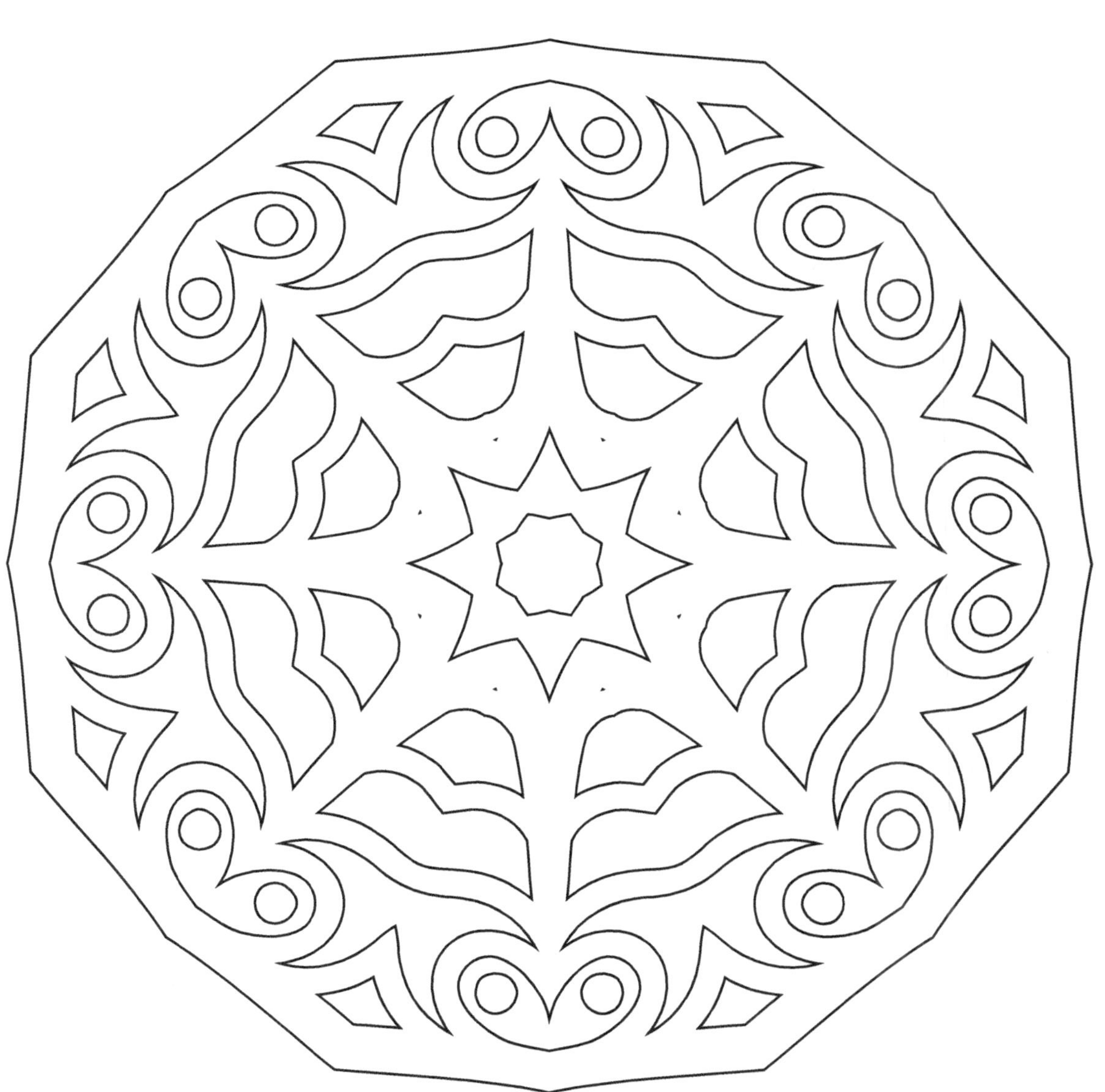

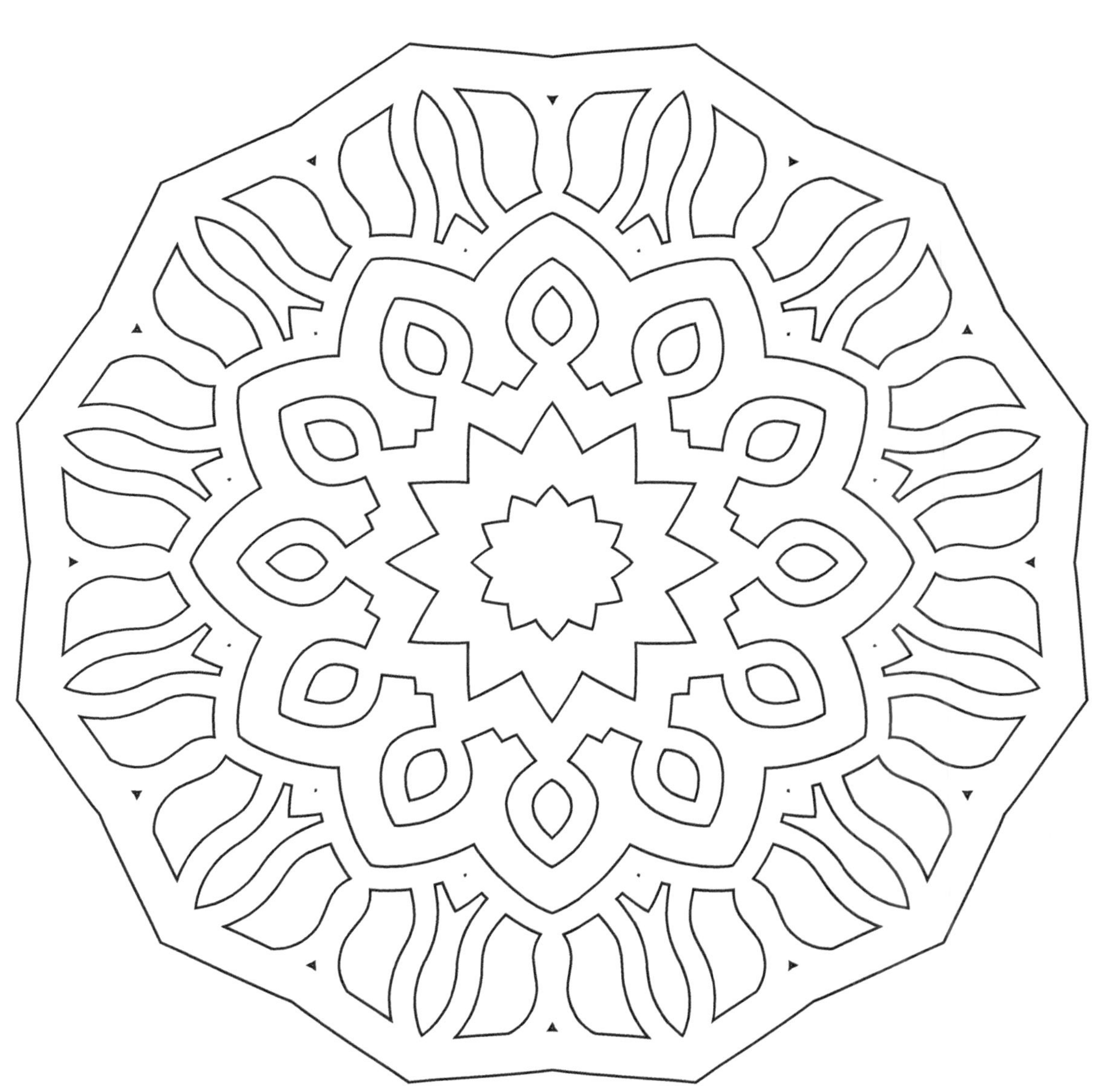

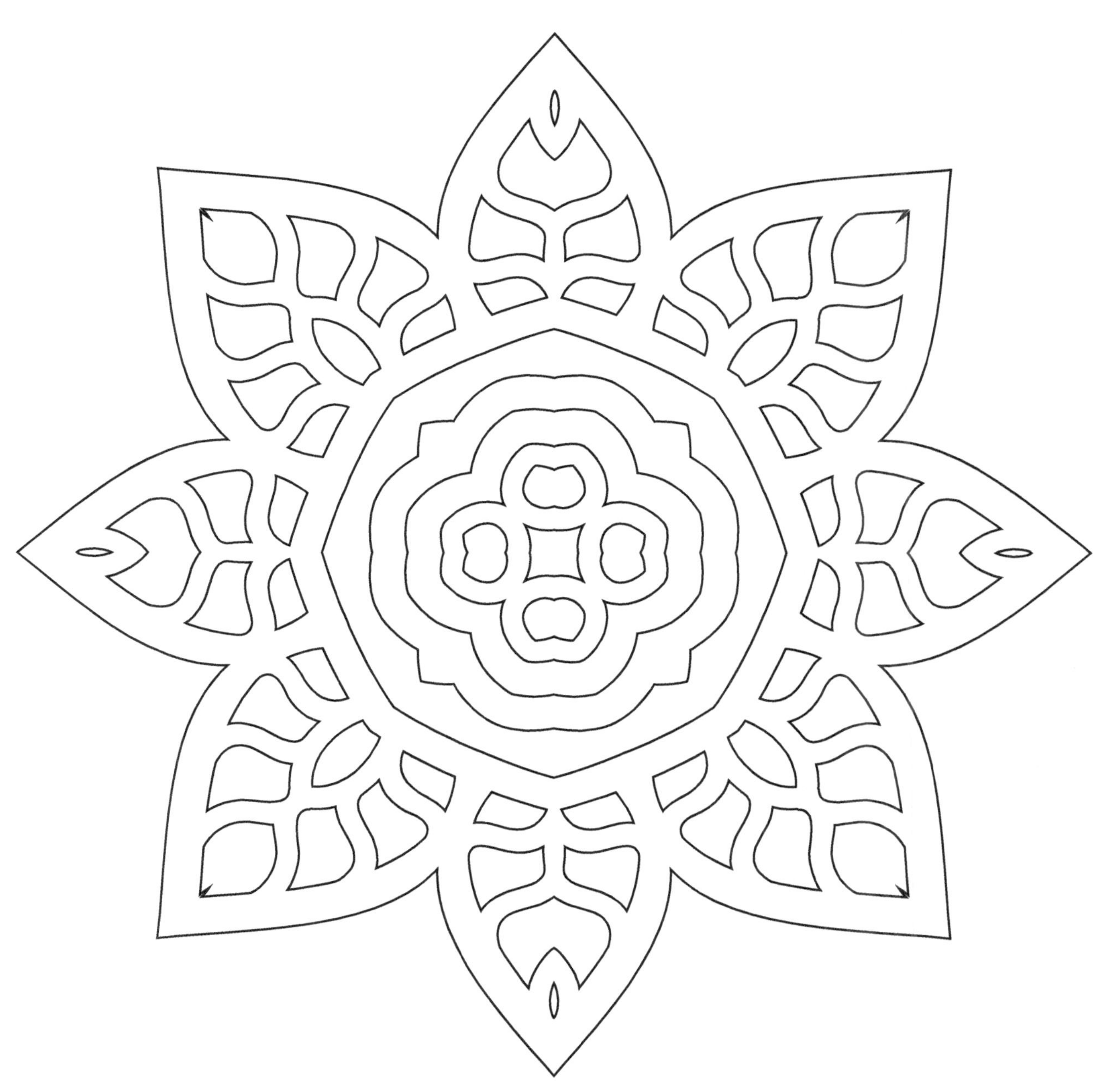

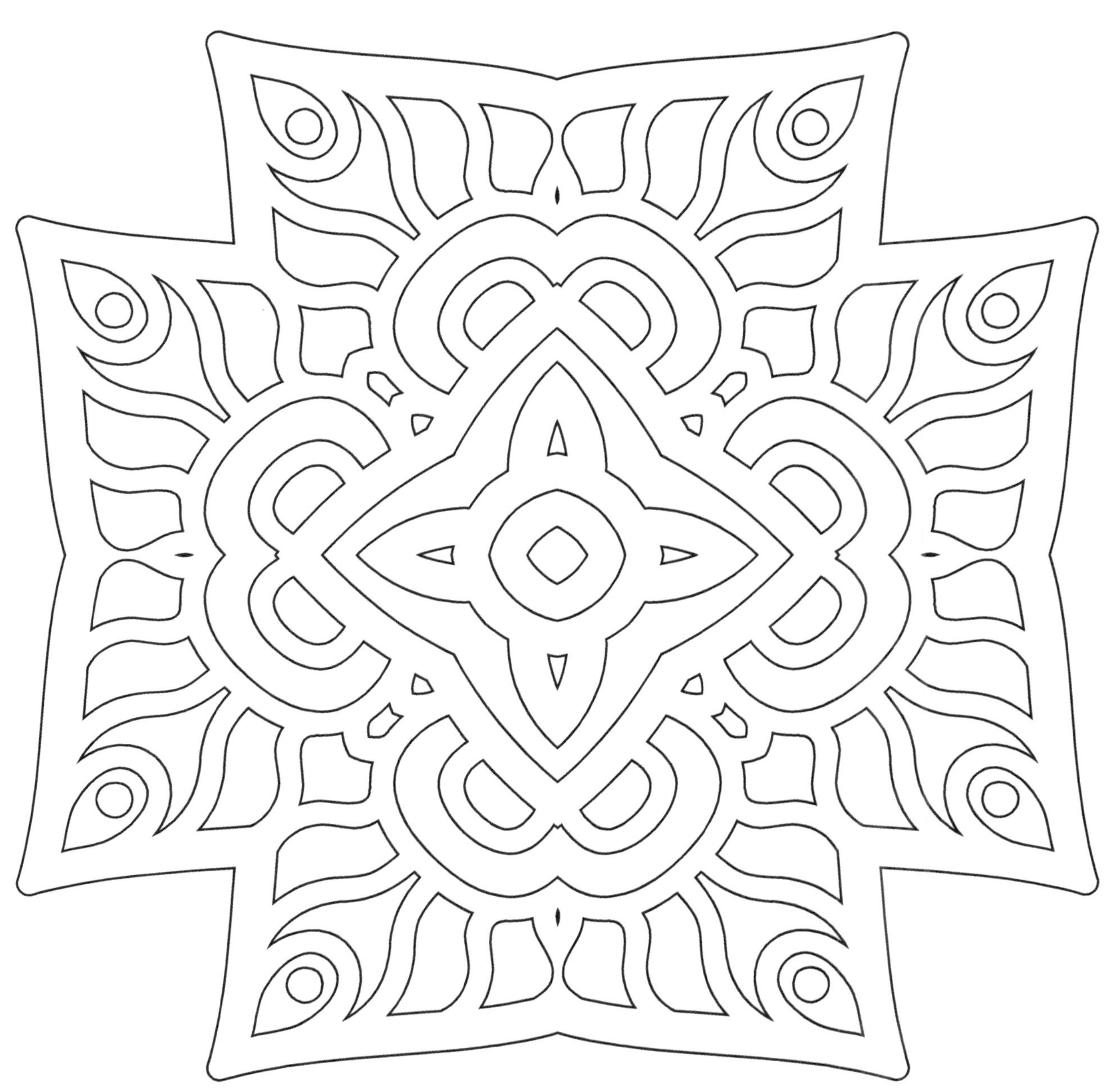

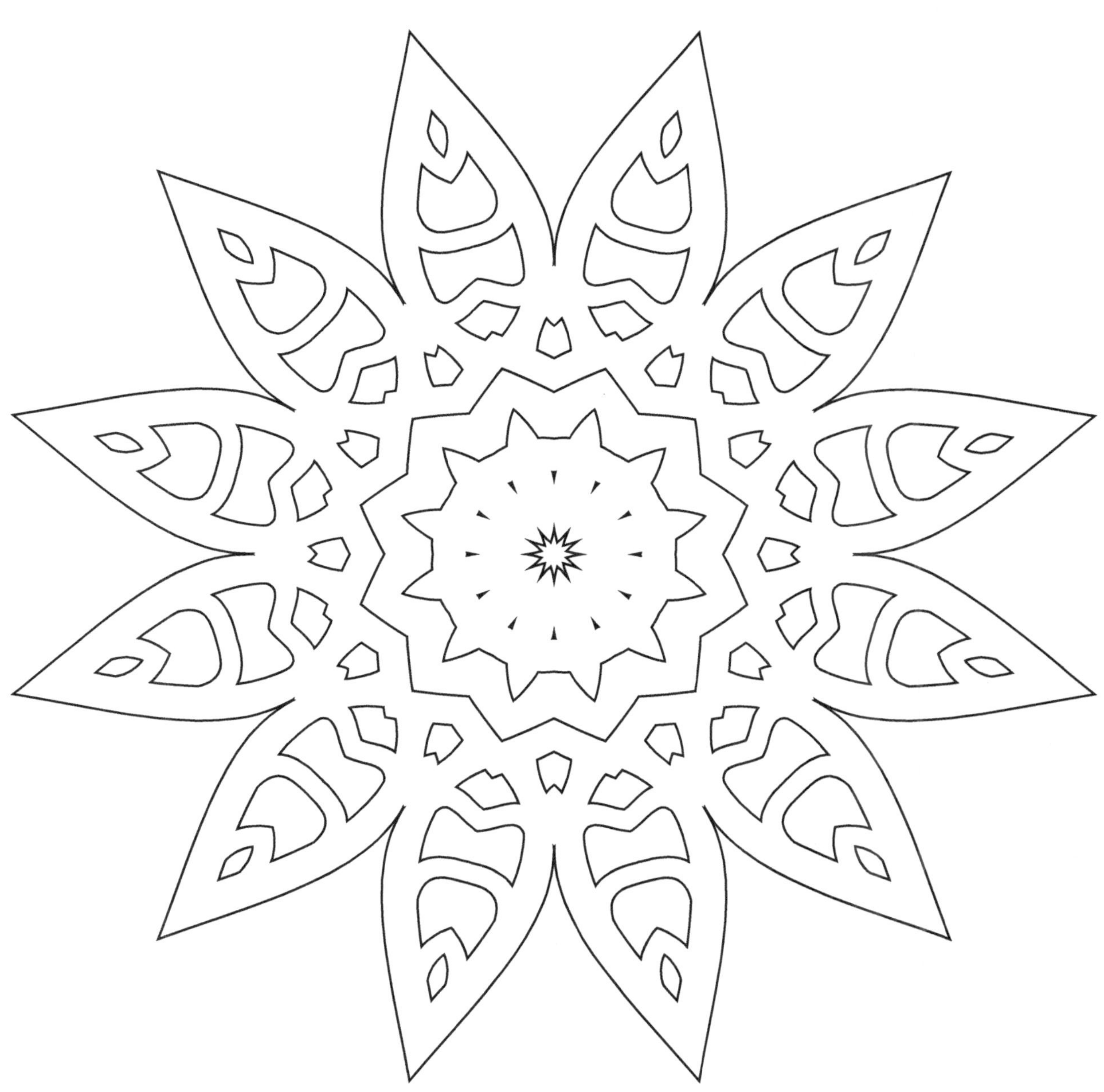

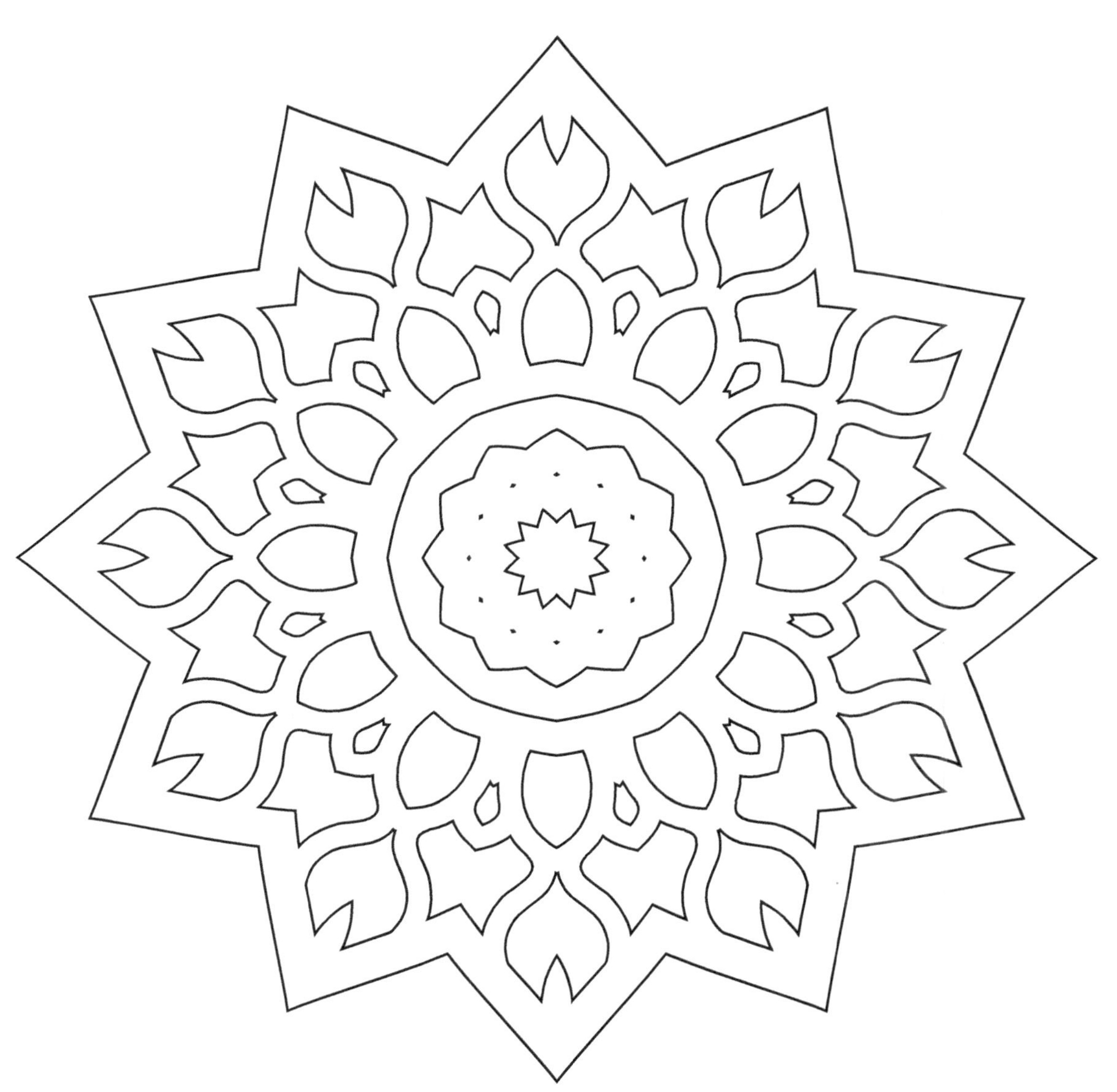

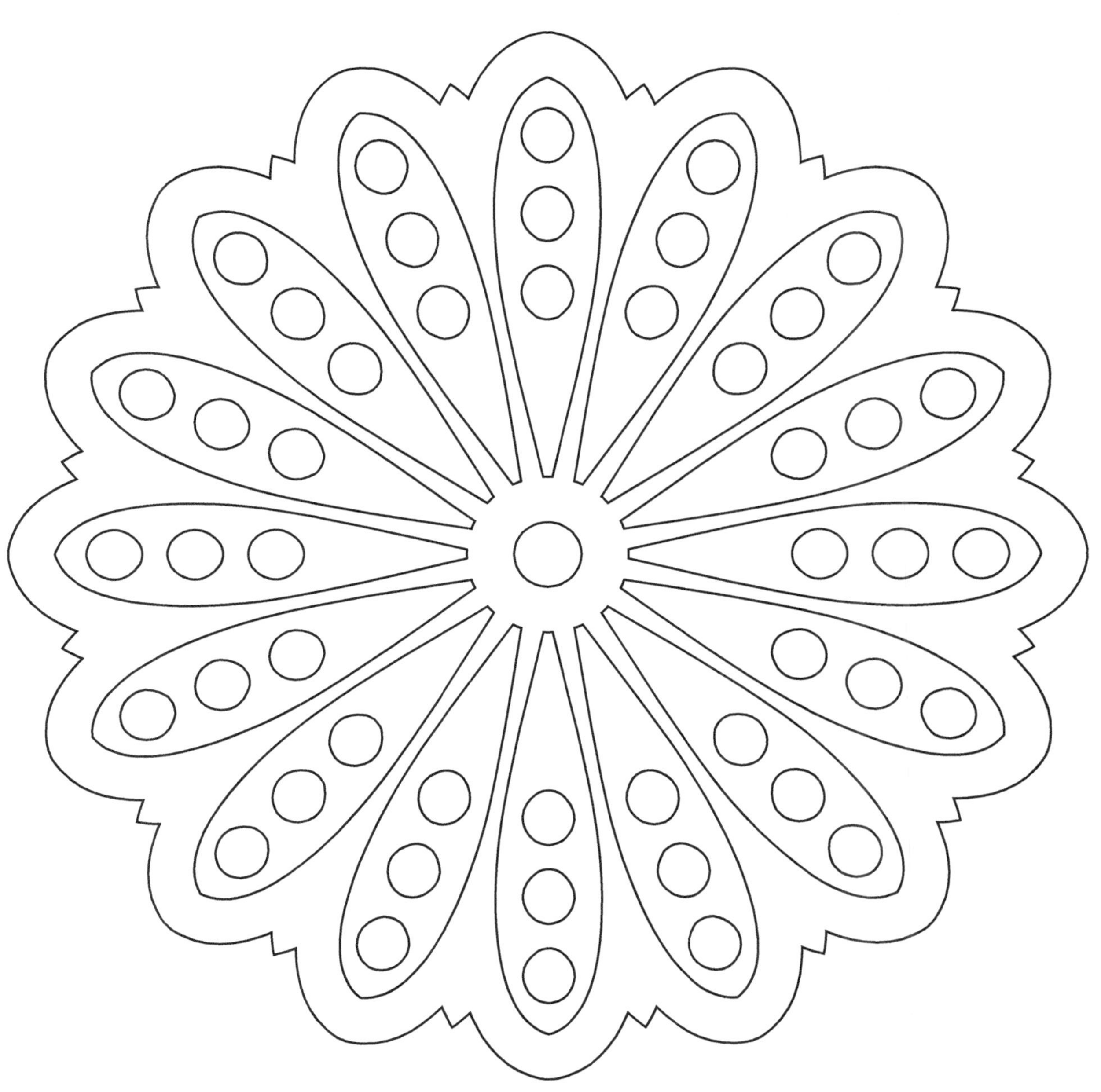

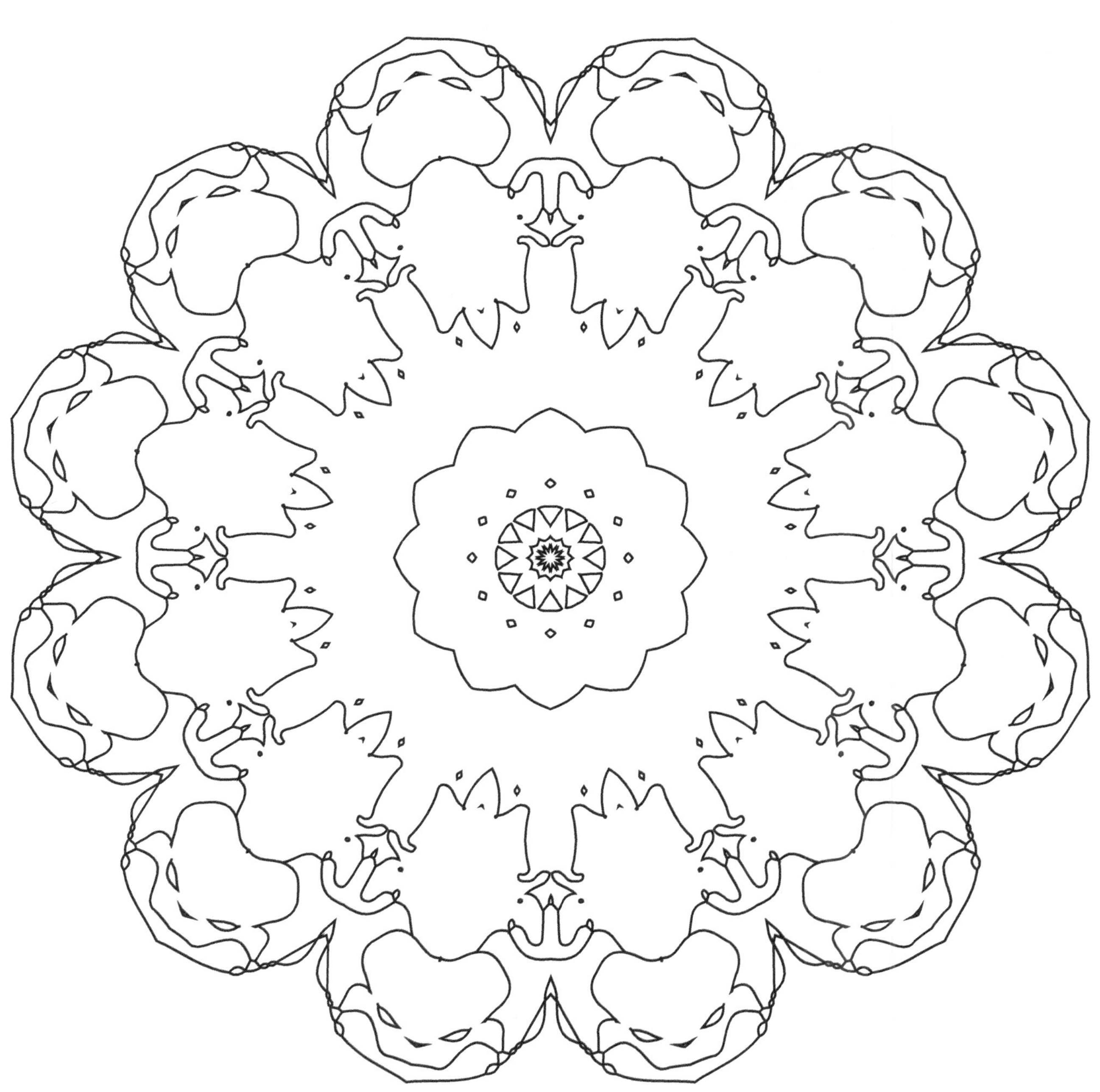

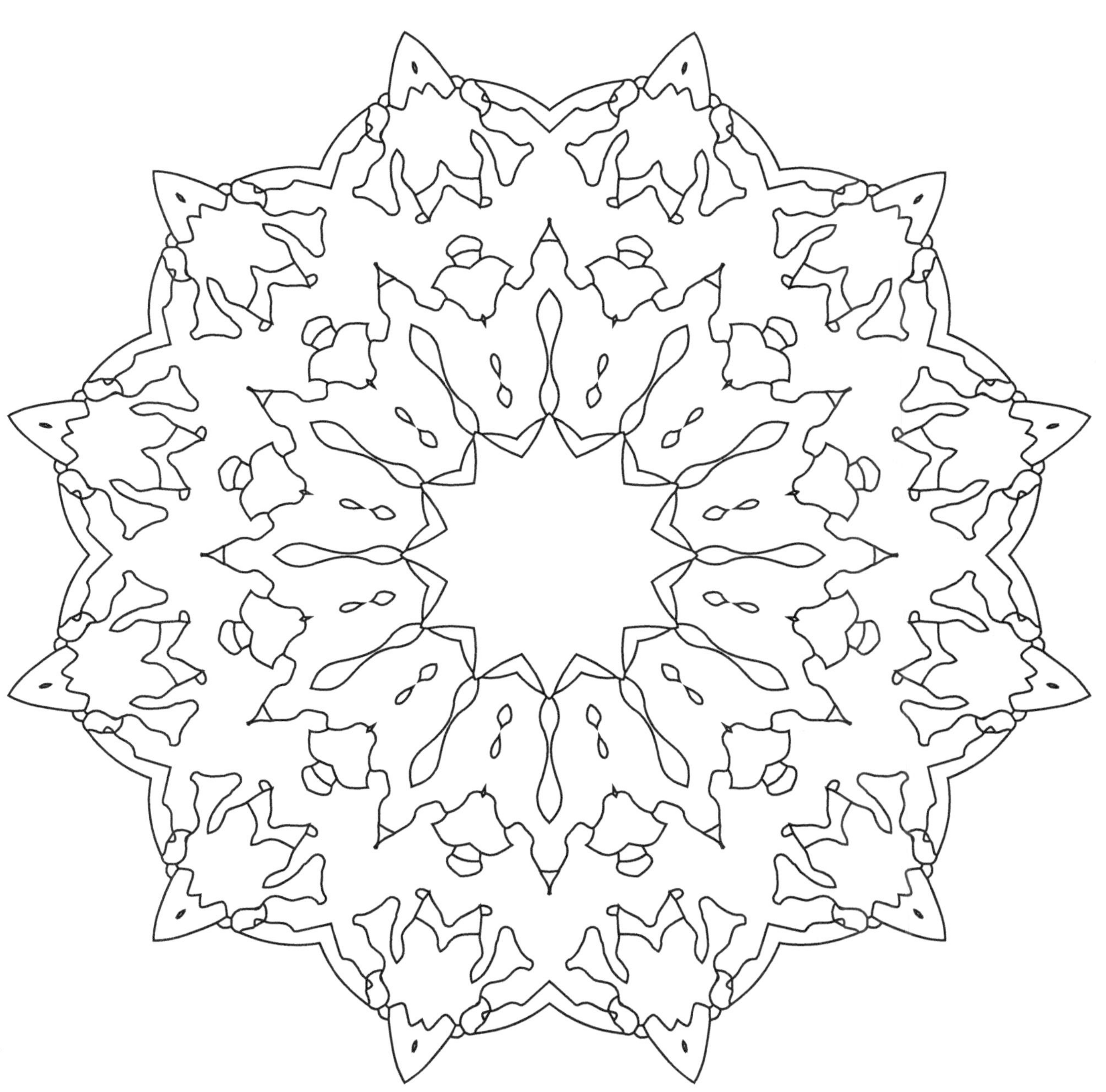

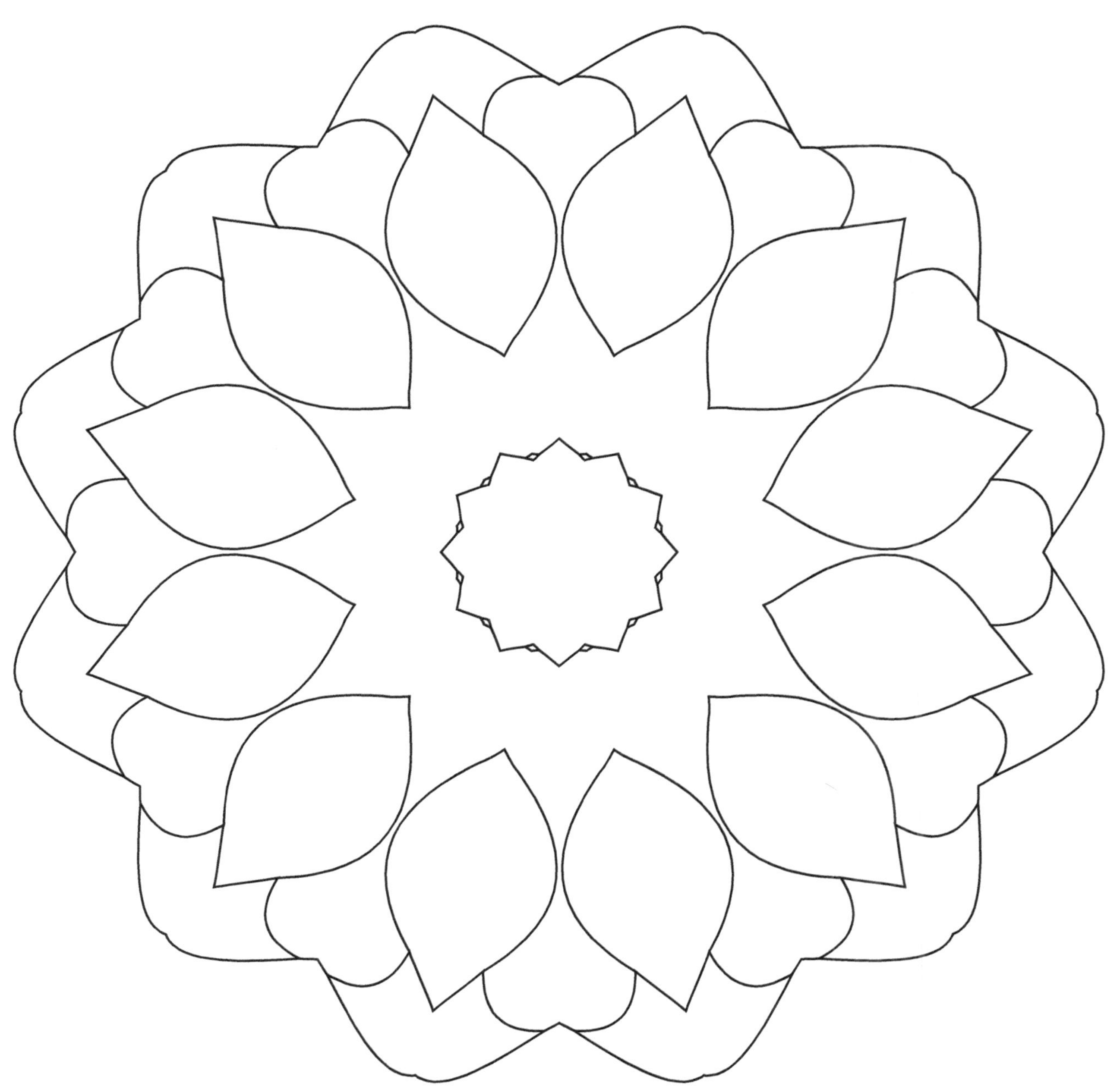

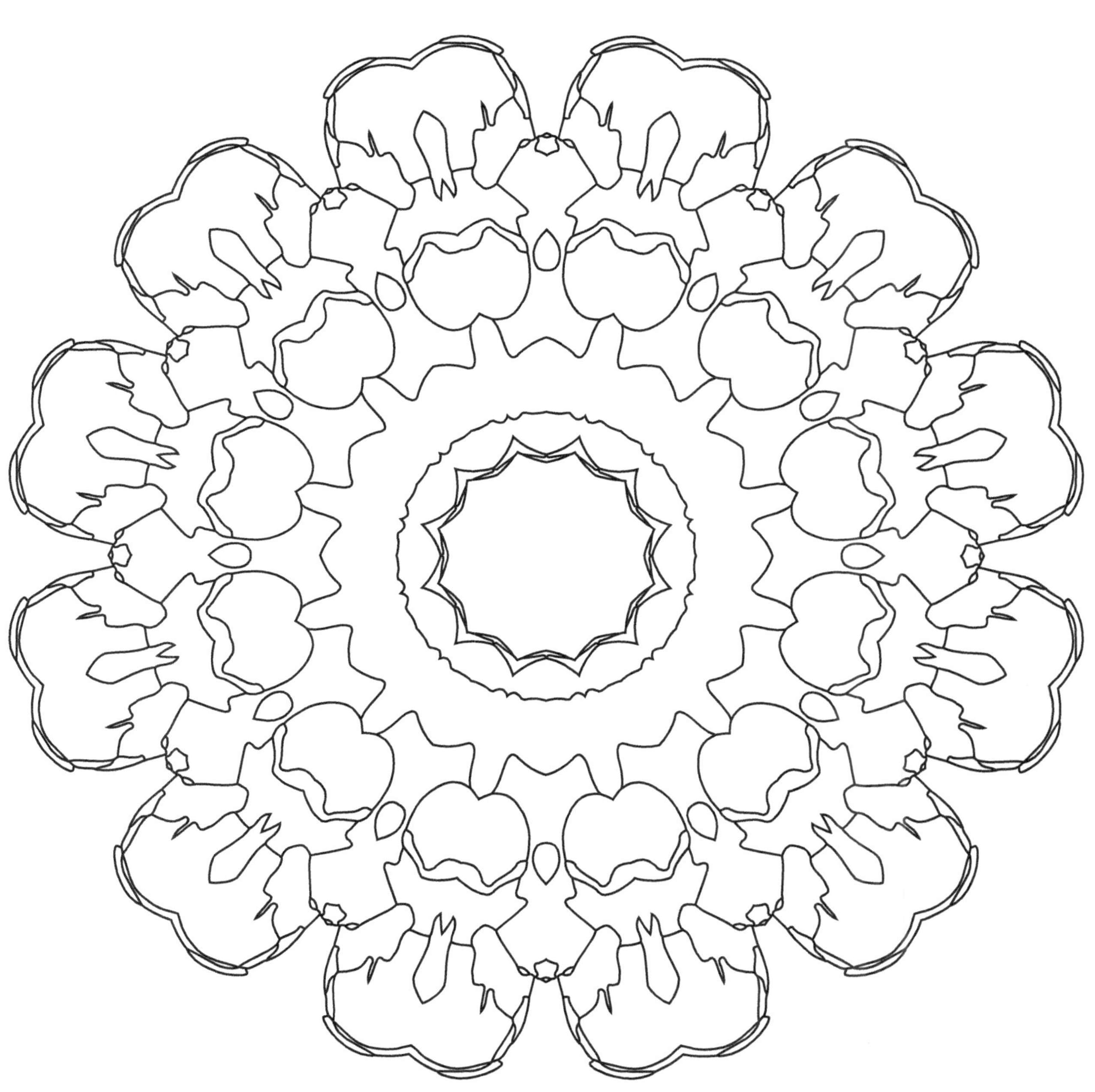

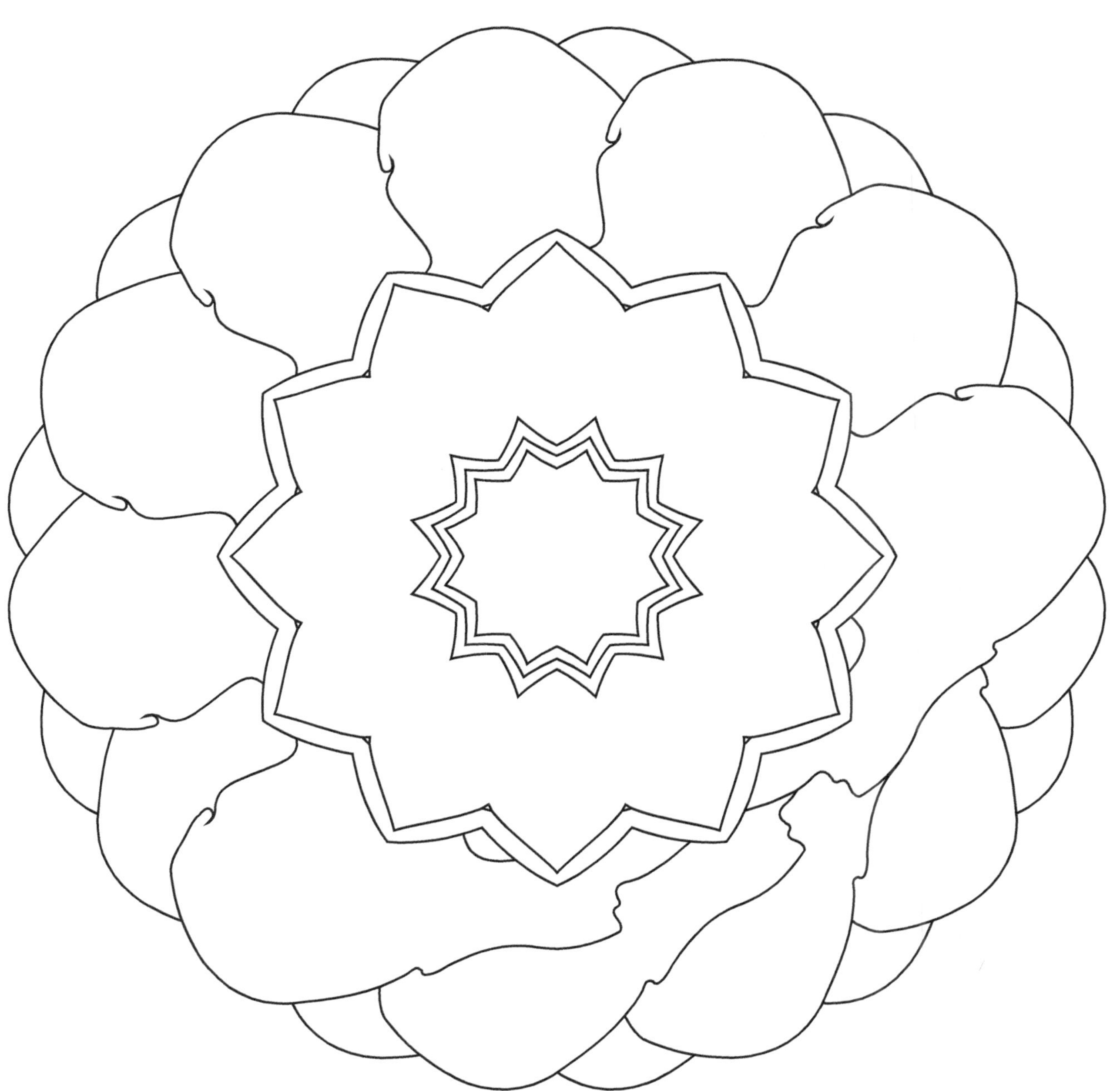

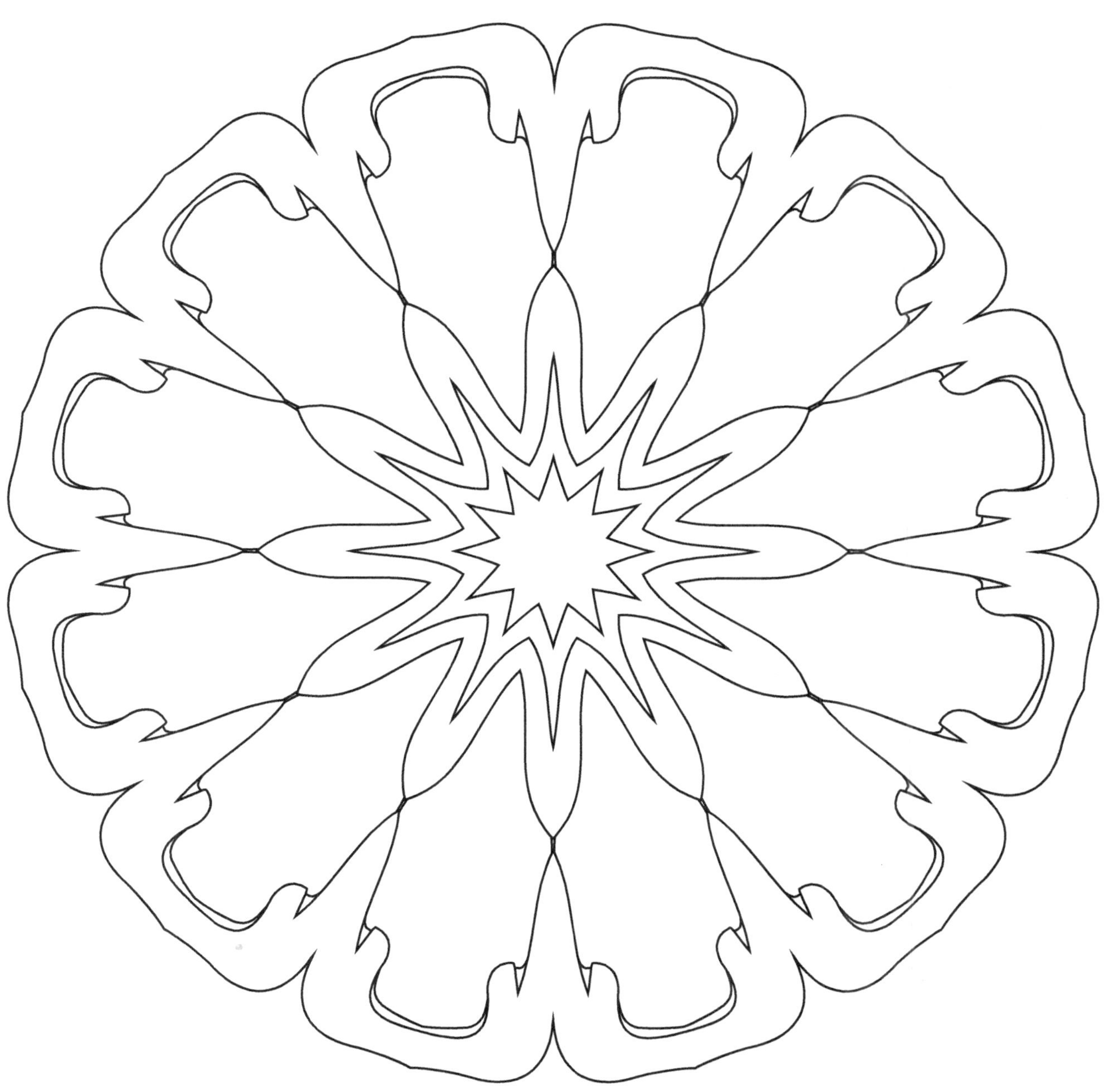

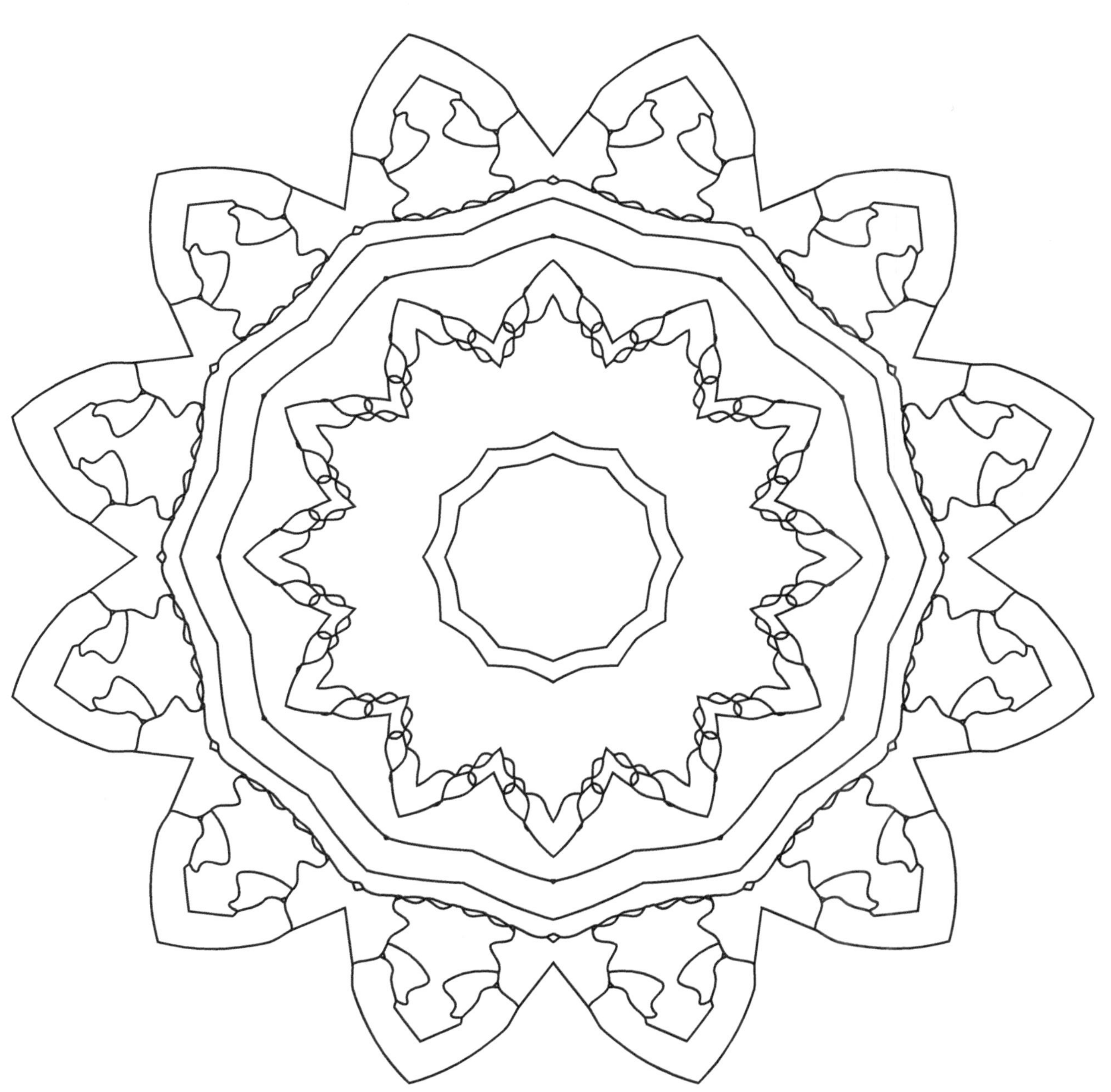

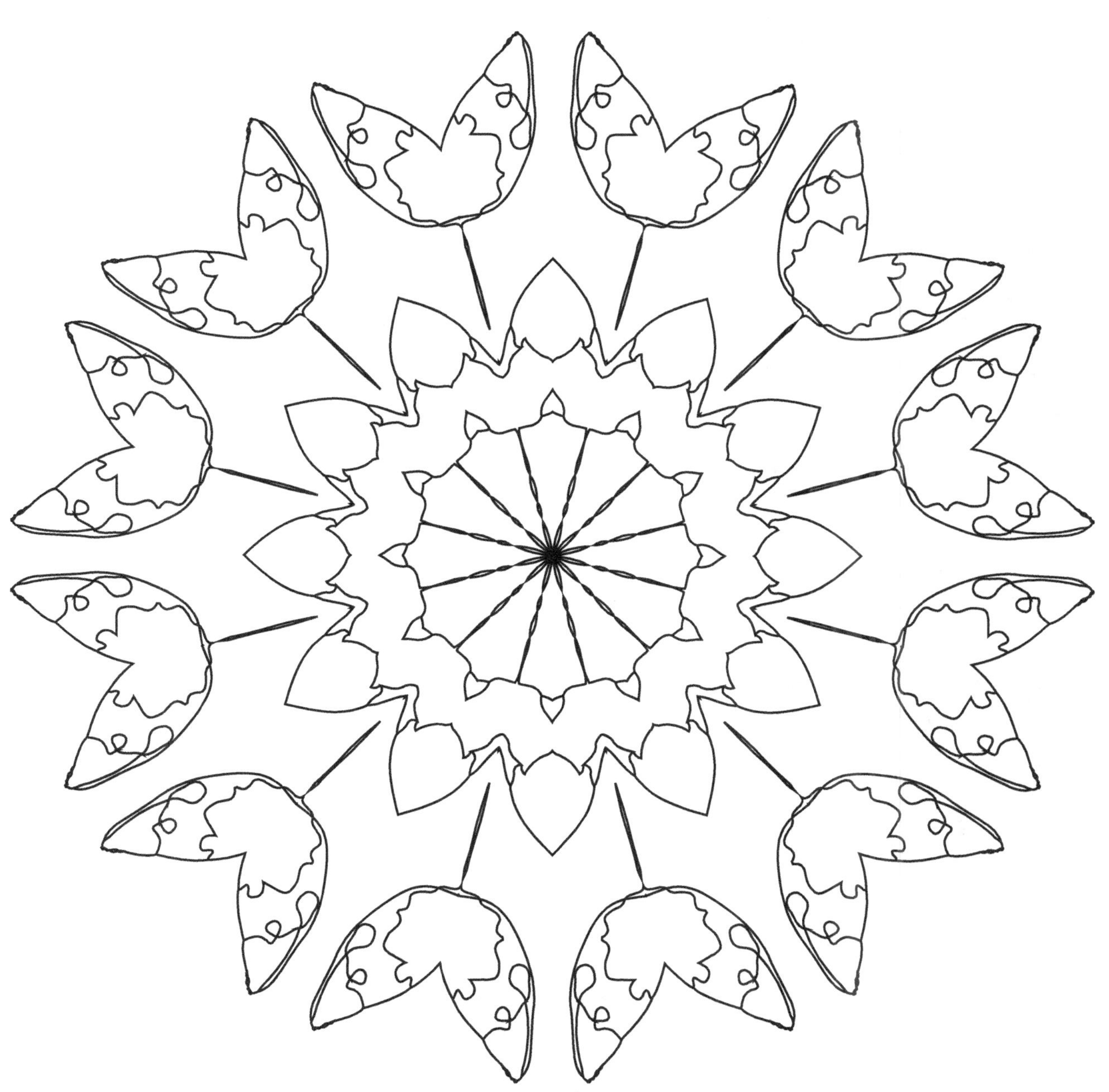

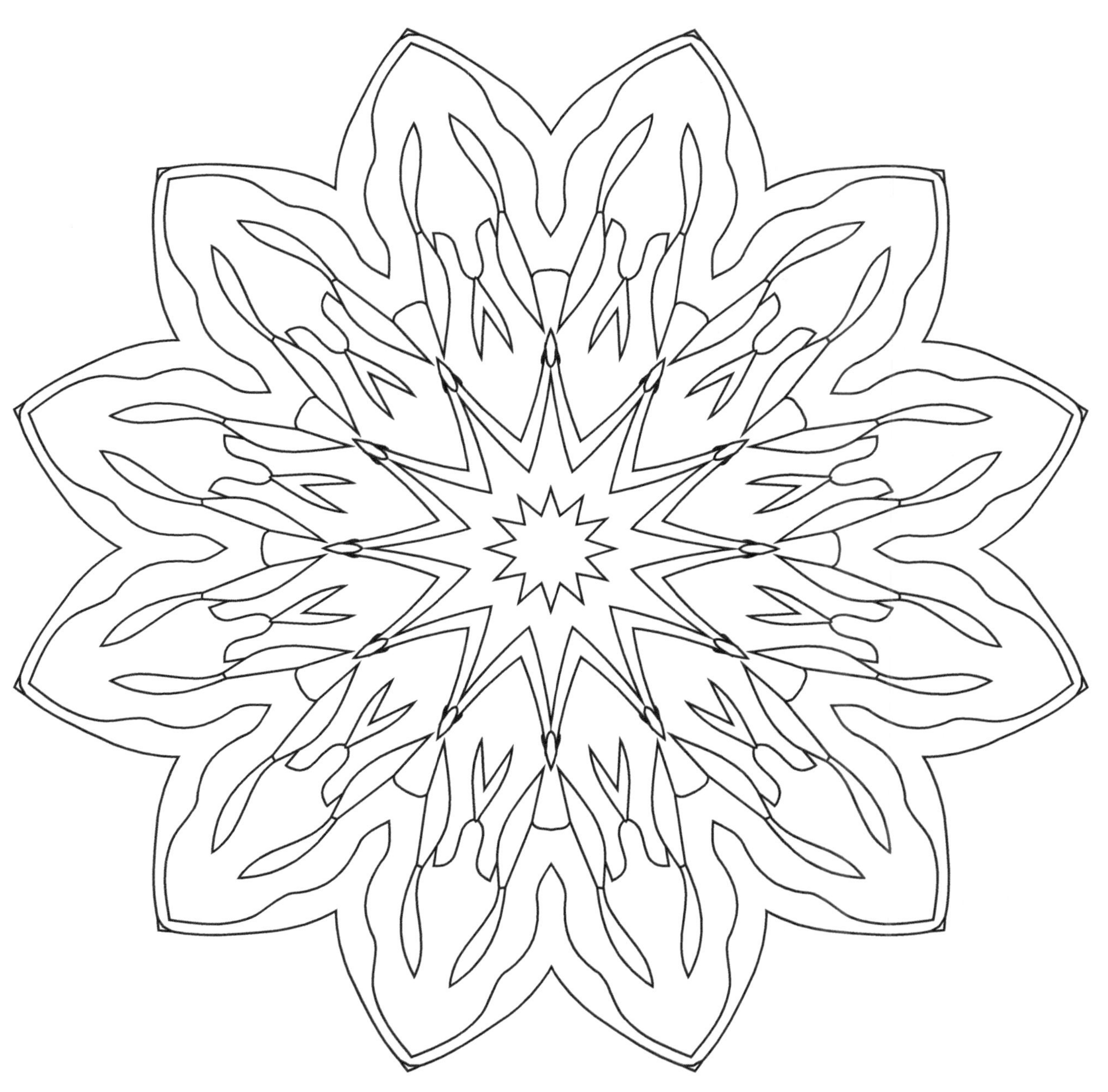

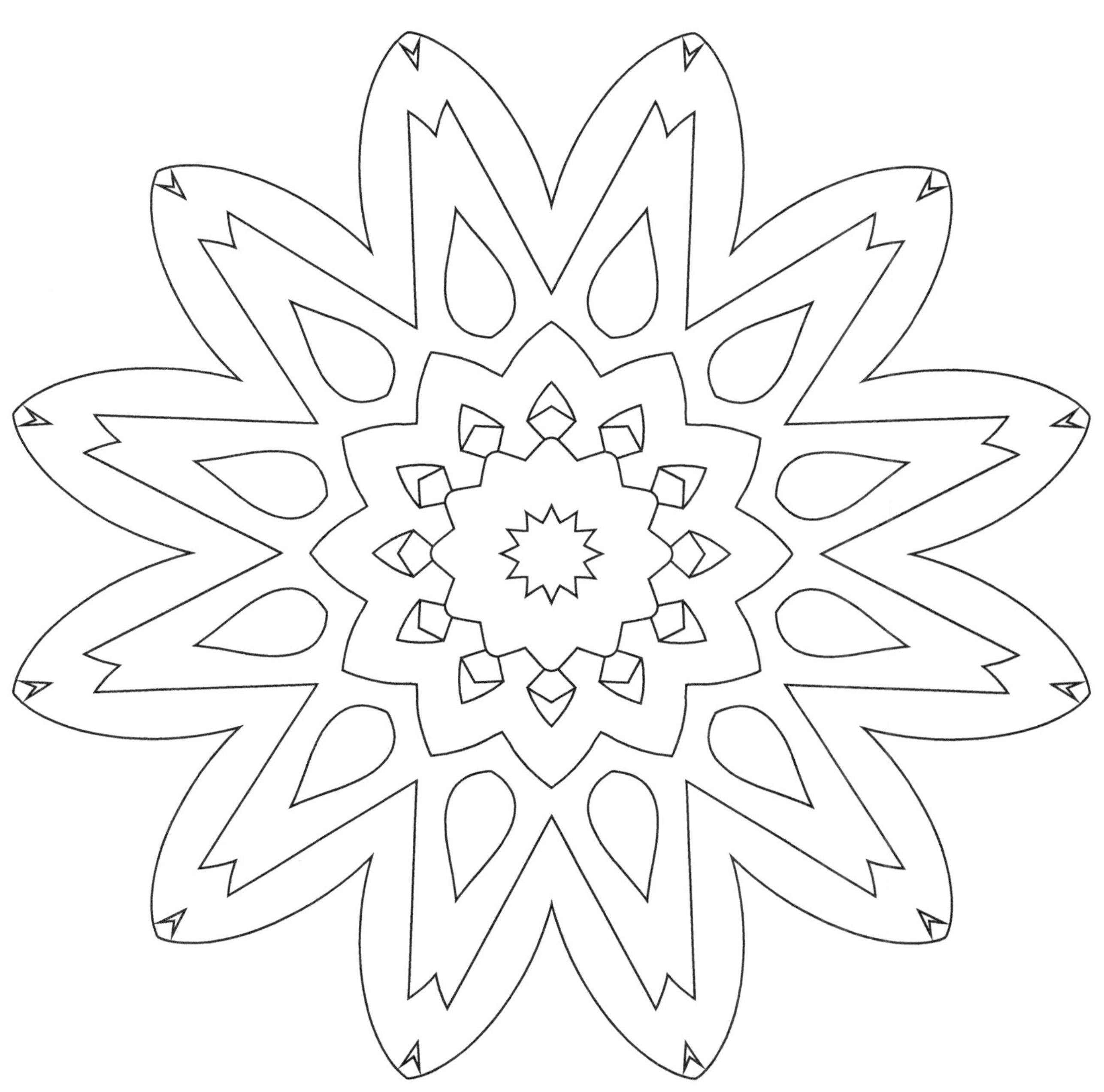

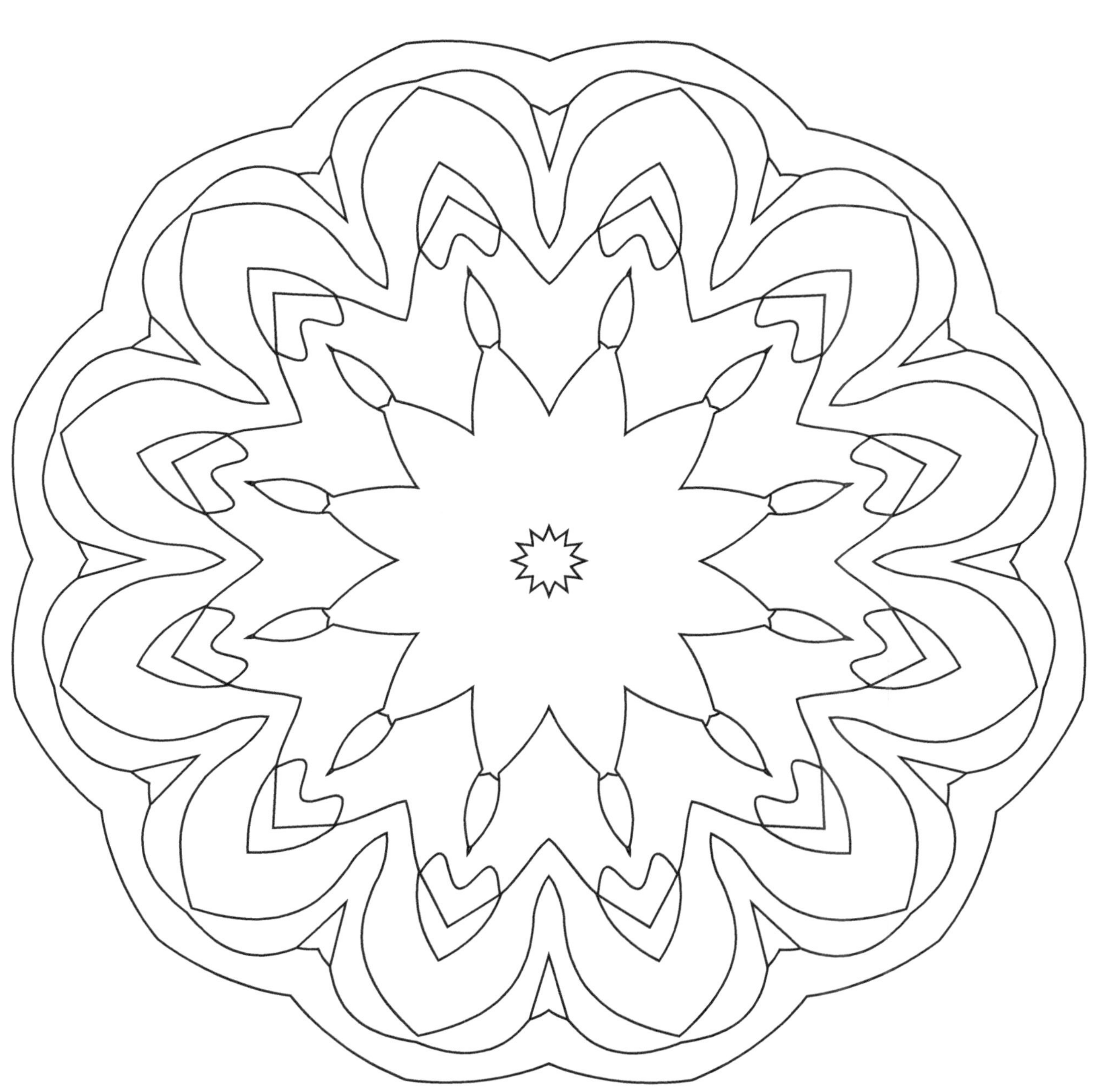

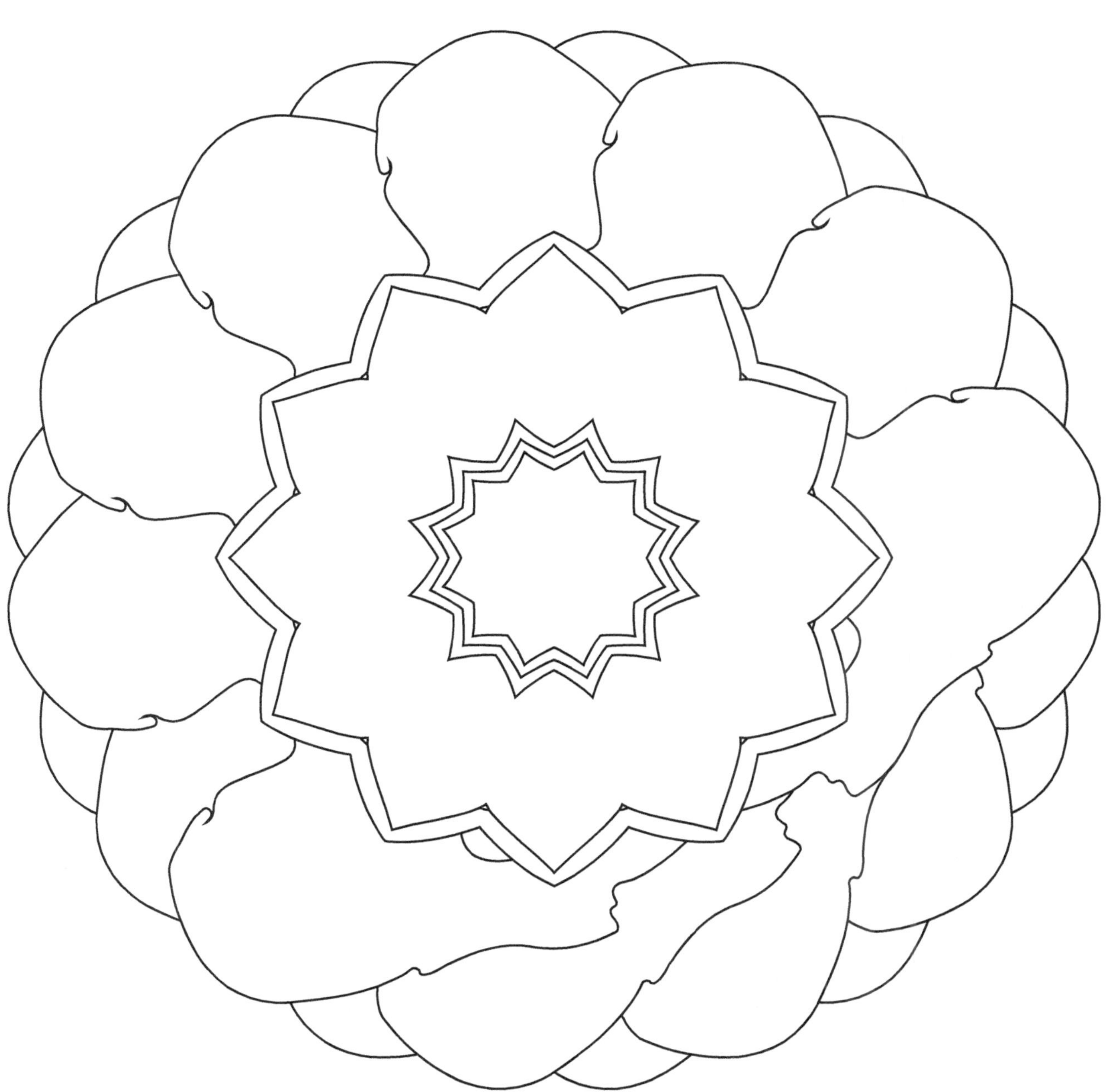

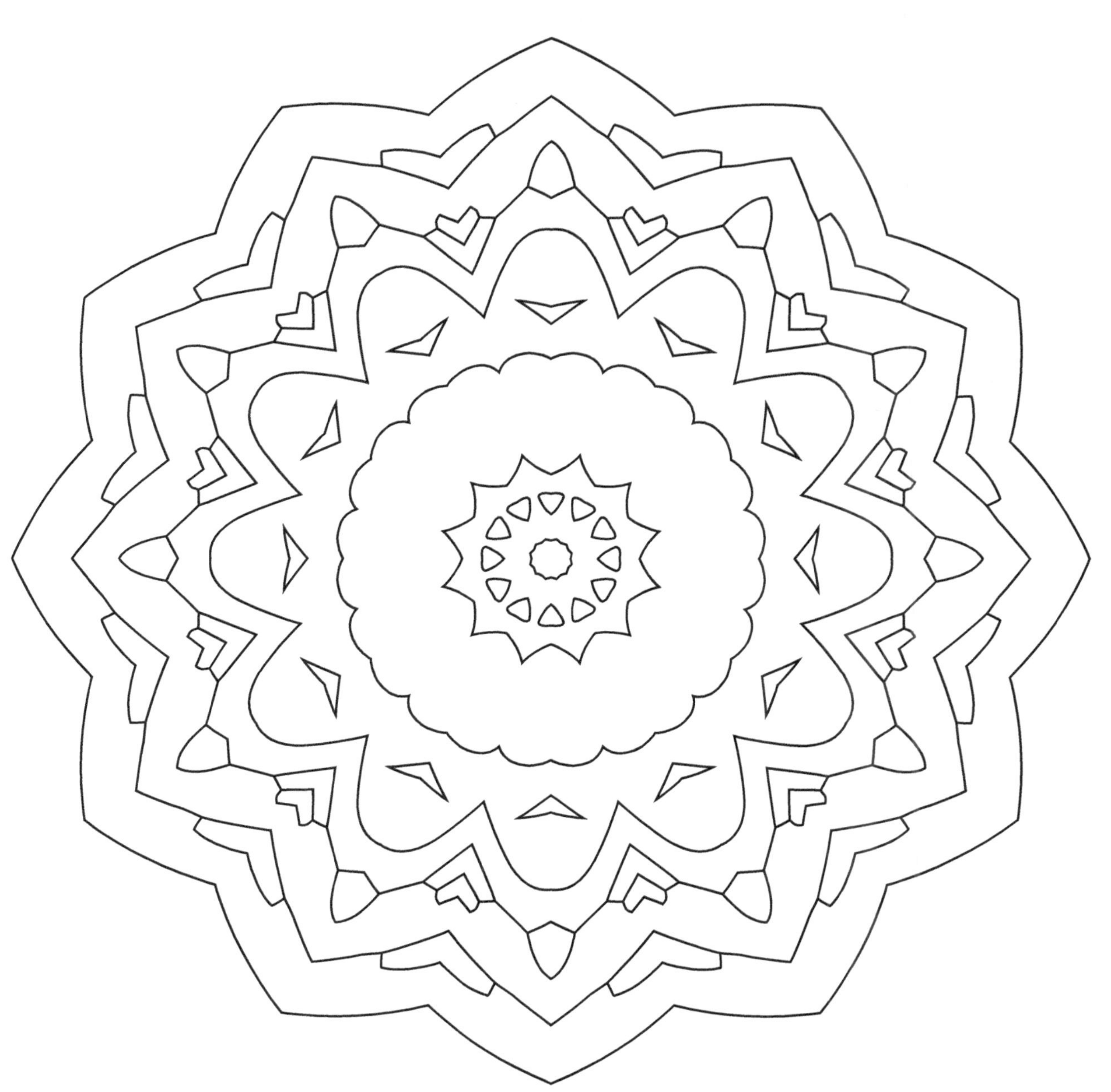

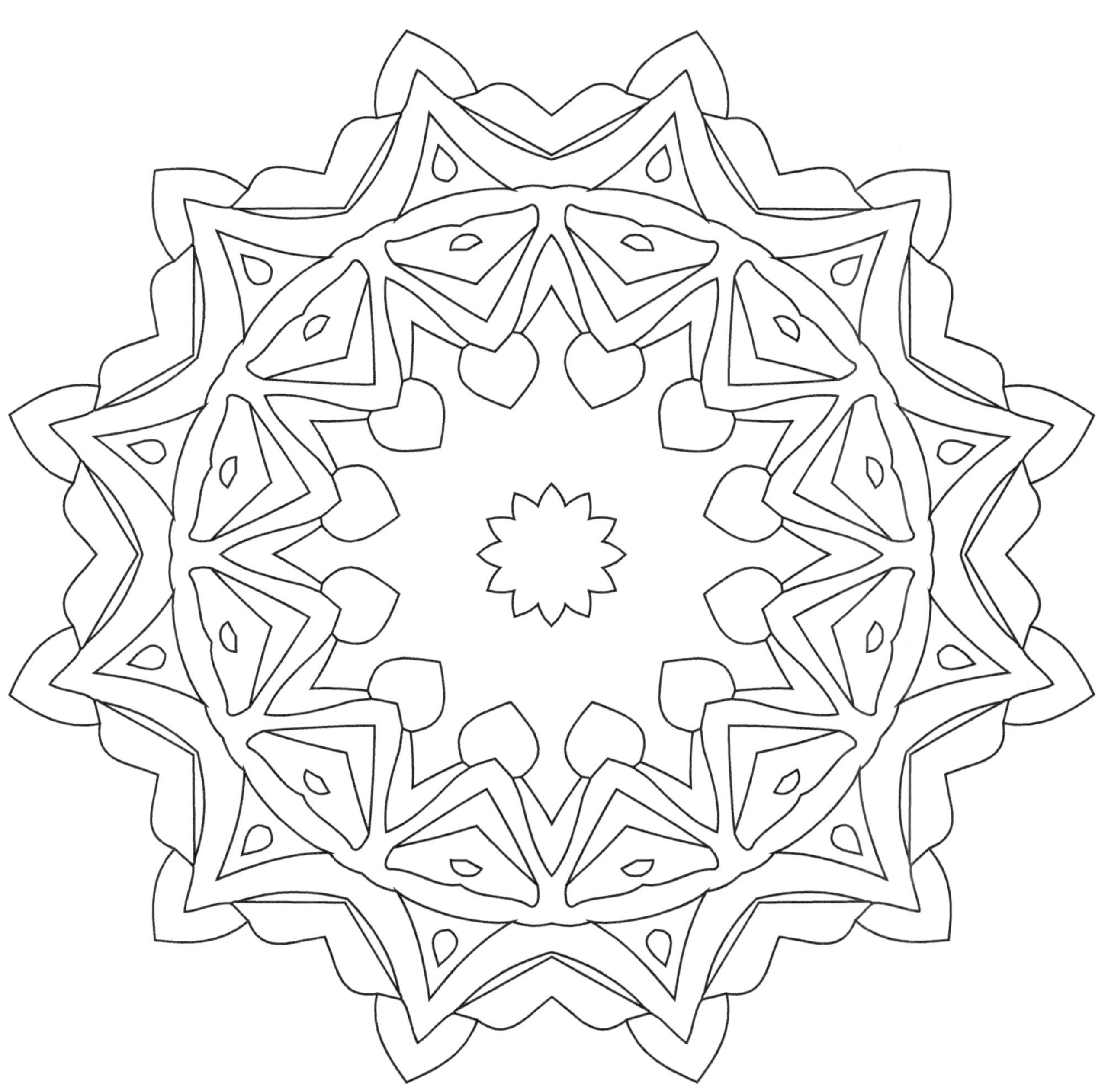

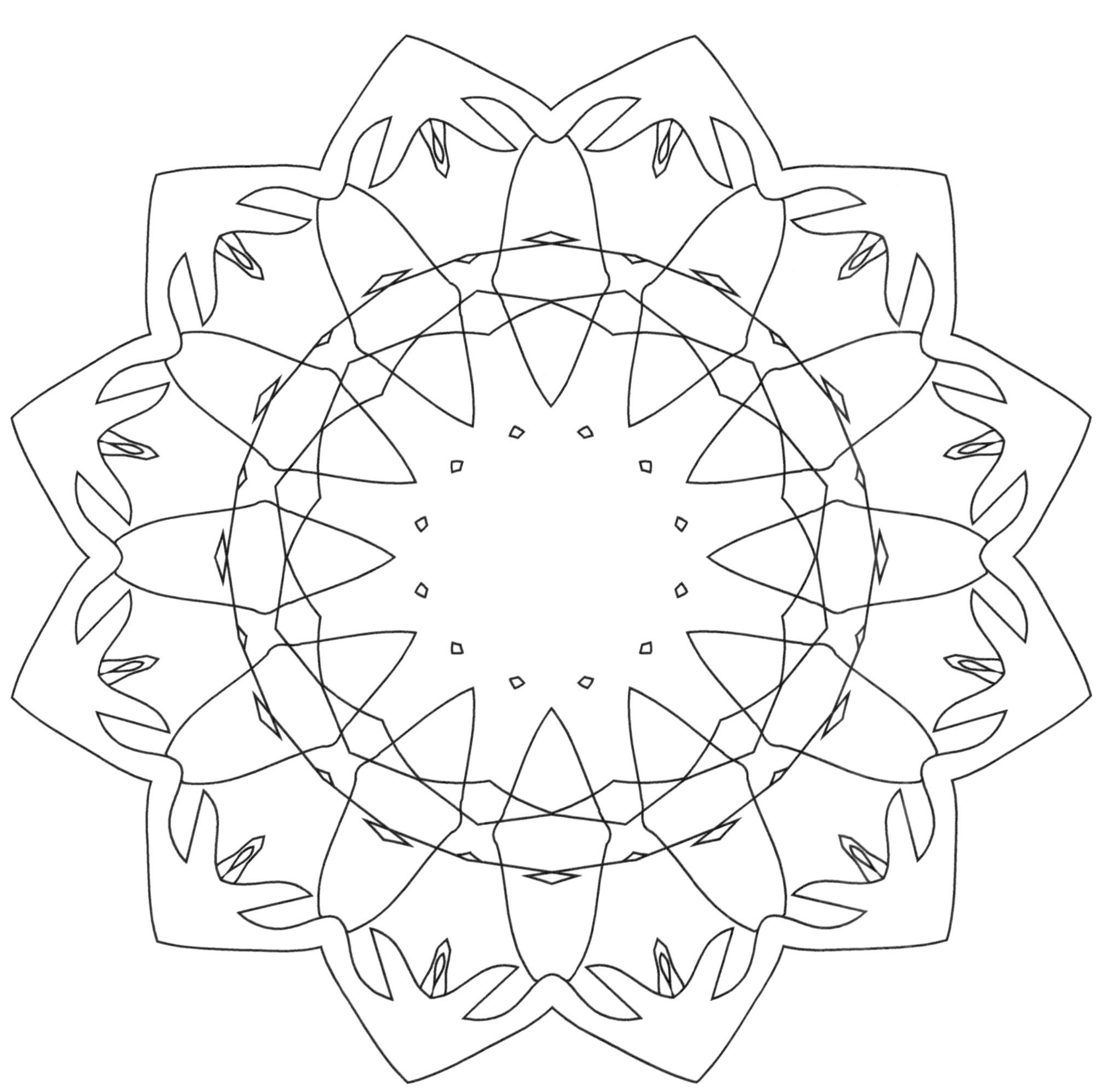

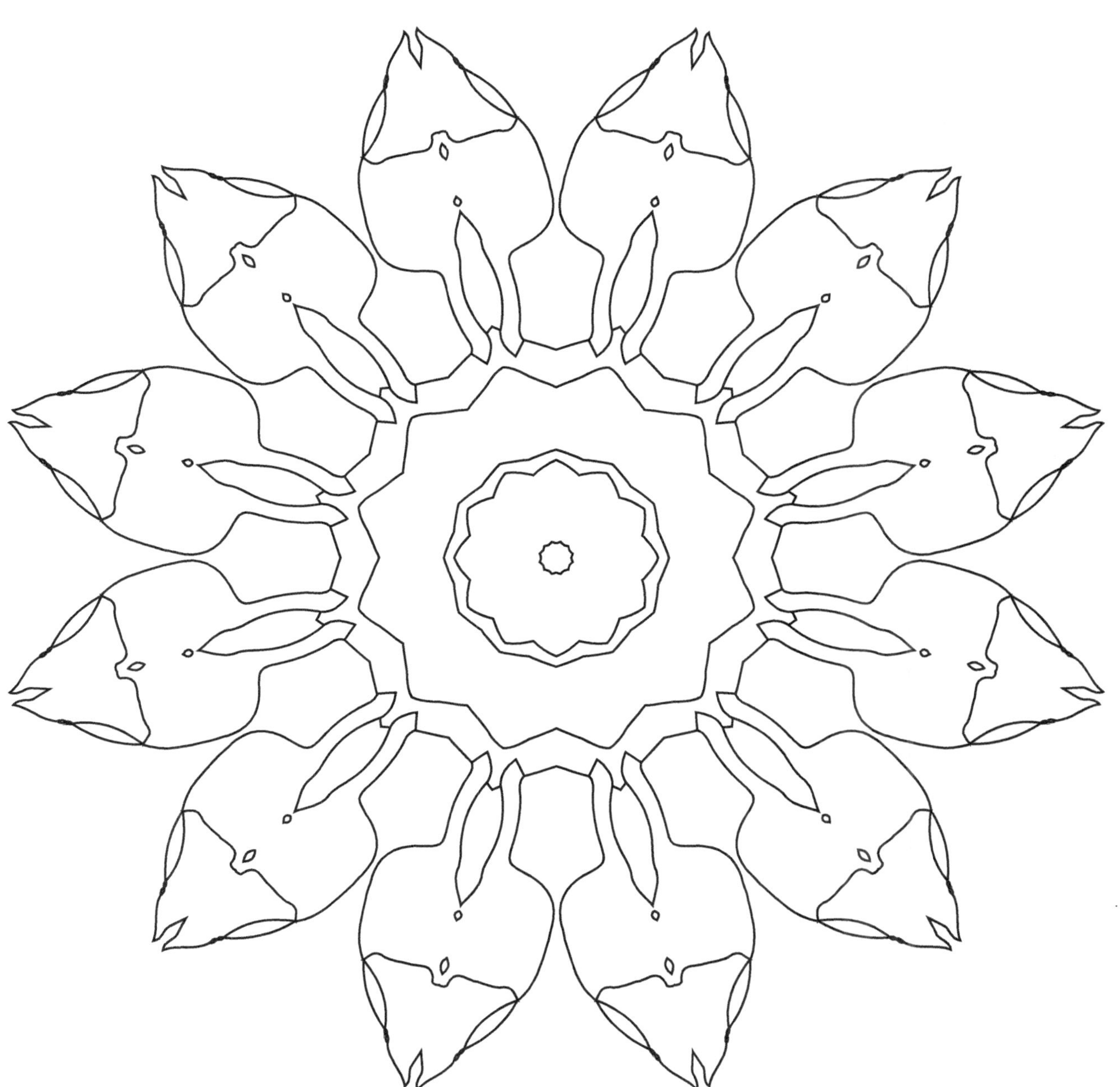

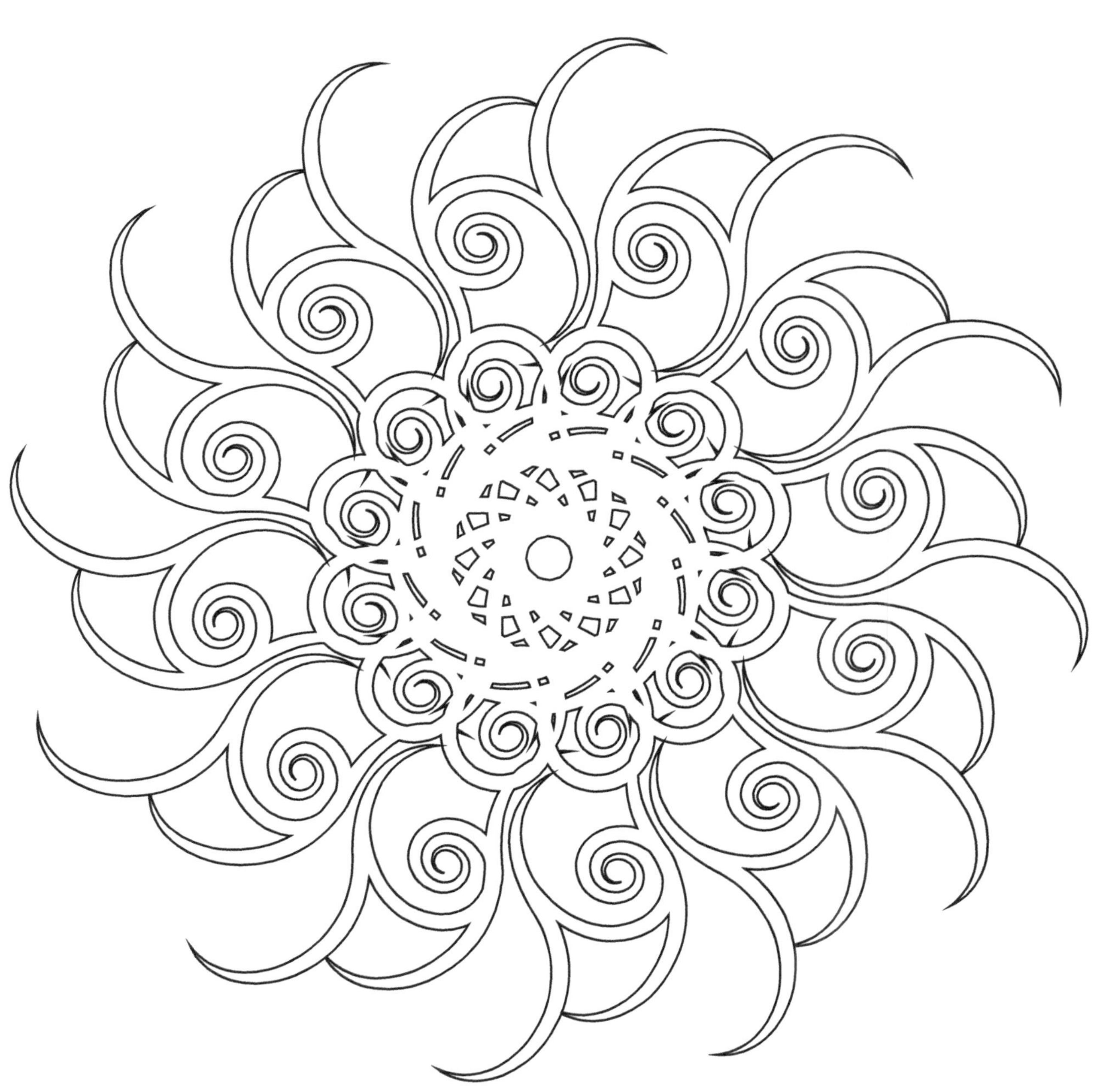

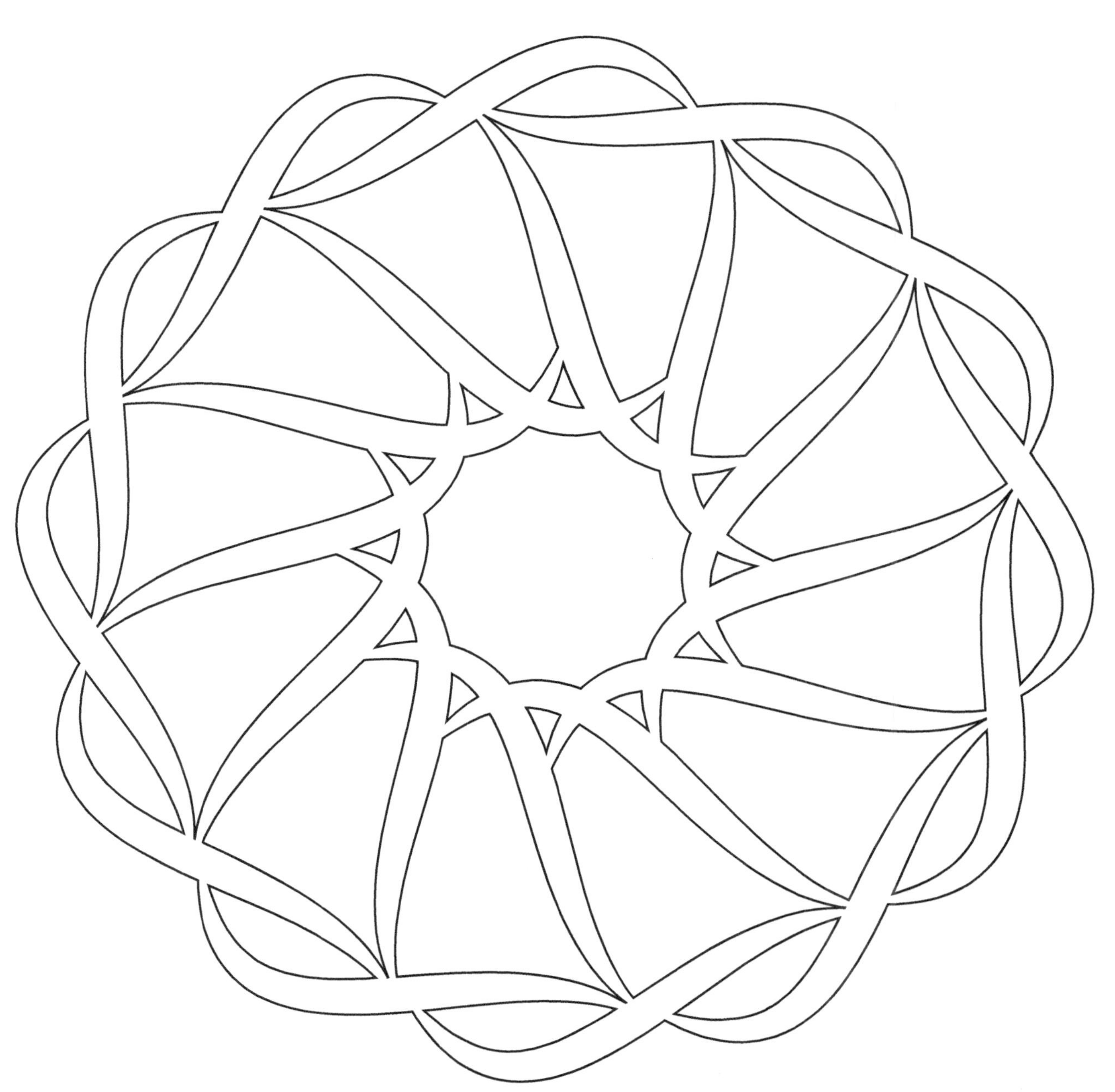

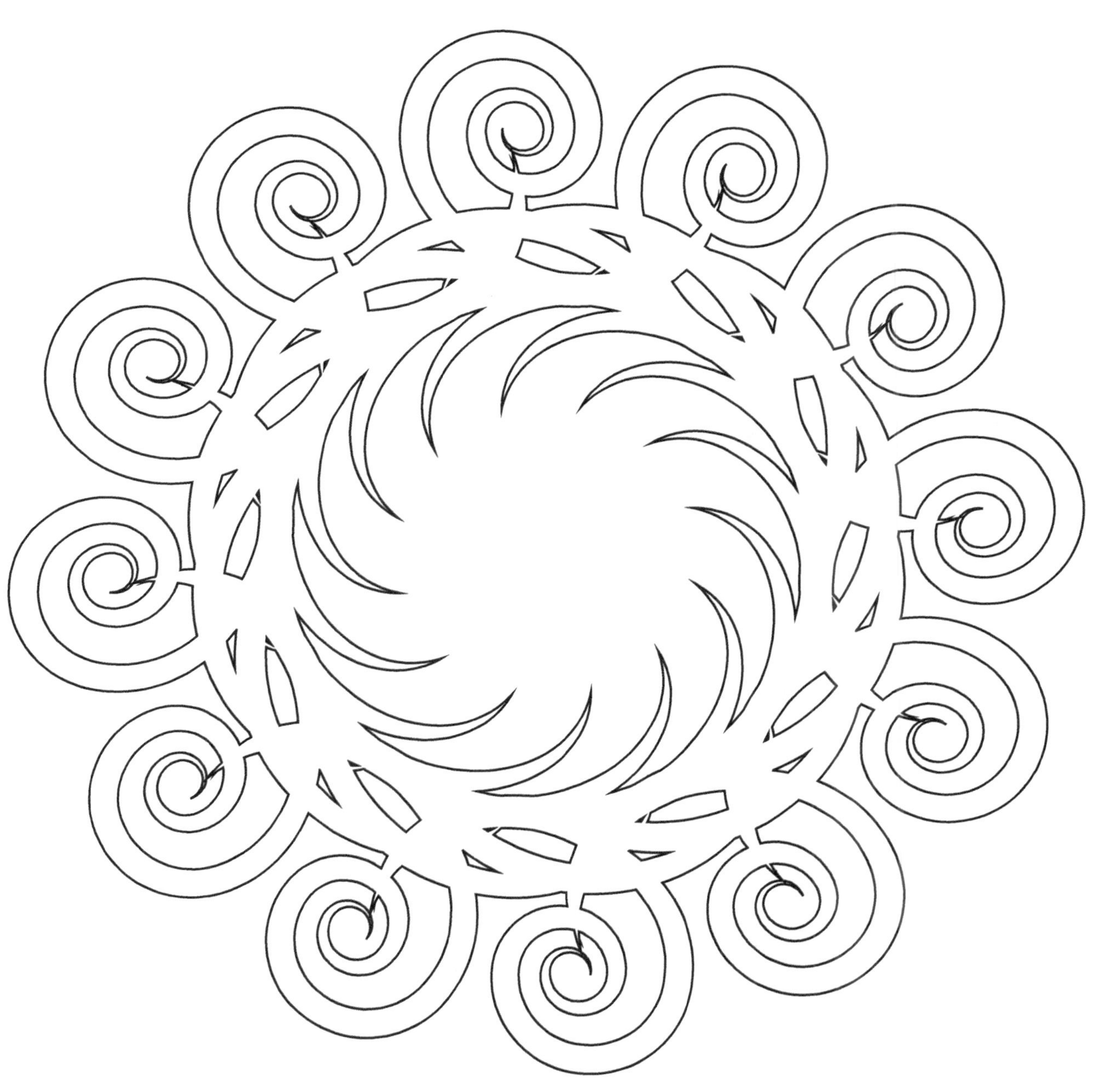

About The
Zen Journal Team

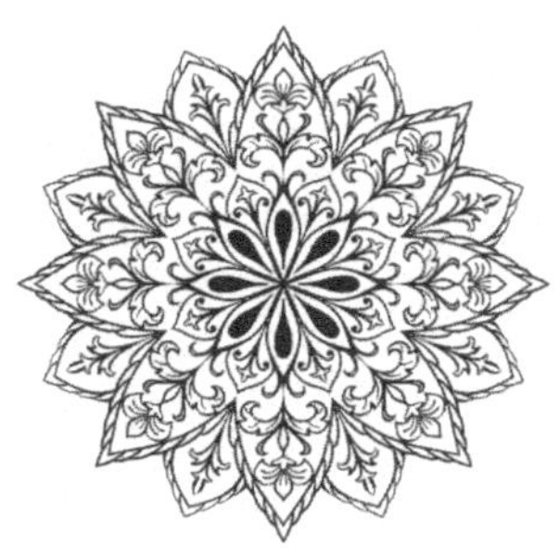

The Zen Journal team prides itself on producing quality themed coloring books for adults.

This latest title "Flower Mandalas Workbook" is an adult coloring book that features the beautiful and mystical side of the latest mandala coloring book craze. Going back in history over a thousand years, Mandalas were and still are today, mystical symbols found in many ancient texts. The guys at Zen have spent many hours developing this basic mystical background into modern flower-like images that are designed to give hours of coloring fun for all members of the family.

Flower Mandalas Workbook (Mandala Coloring Books For Adults) is the third in a planned twenty book collection of Mandala coloring books known simply as the Magical Artwork Designs series.

Visit us online to download more Mandala Coloring Pages and to see our full range of Mandala Coloring Books:

www.ZenArtworkMandalas.com